# The Triangle Area

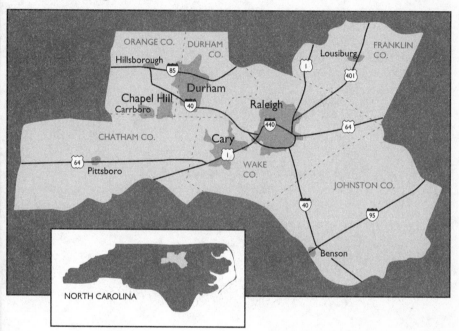

ORANGE CO.   DURHAM CO.   FRANKLIN CO.

Hillsborough   Lousiburg

Durham

Chapel Hill   Raleigh

Carrboro

CHATHAM CO.   Cary

WAKE CO.

Pittsboro

JOHNSTON CO.

Benson

NORTH CAROLINA

## Other Trail Books by the Author

*Hiking and Backpacking* (1979, 1983, 1989, 1994)
*North Carolina Hiking Trails* (1982, 1988, 1996)
*The Trails of Virginia: Hiking the Old Dominion* (1984, 1995)
*South Carolina Trails* (1984, 1989, 1994)
*Hiking and Backpacking Basics* (1985, 1992)
*Hiking the Mountain State: The Trails of West Virginia* (1986, 1997)
*Monongahela National Forest Hiking Guide* (1988, 1993)
*Adventuring in Florida, Georgia Sea Islands and Okefenokee Swamp*
    (1991, 1995)
*Trails of the Triad* (1997)

# TRAILS
# OF THE
# TRIANGLE

Over 200 Hikes in the Raleigh/
Durham/ Chapel Hill Area

## Allen de Hart

John F. Blair, Publisher   Winston-Salem, North Carolina

The paper in this book meets the guidelines
for permanence and durability of the
Committee on Production Guidelines for
Book Longevity of the Council on Library Resources.

**Cover photographs (clockwise from left):
Duke Chapel in Durham, Old Well at UNC in Chapel Hill,
Bell Tower at NC State University in Raleigh. Photos courtesy
of NC Travel and Tourism Division, Raleigh, NC.**

Design, maps, and composition by Liza Langrall
All photographs by author unless otherwise noted
Printed and bound by R. R. Donnelley and Sons, Inc.

Library of Congress Cataloging-in-Publication Data:
De Hart, Allen.
Trails of the Triangle : over 200 hikes in the Raleigh/Durham/
Chapel Hill area / Allen de Hart
p.      cm.
Includes index.
ISBN 0-89587-160-2 (alk. paper)
1. Hiking—North Carolina—Raleigh Metropolitan Area—Guidebooks.
2. Hiking—North Carolina—Durham Metropolitan Area—Guidebooks.
3. Hiking—North Carolina—Chapel Hill Metropolitan Area—Guidebooks.
4. Trails—North Carolina—Raleigh Metropolitan Area—Guidebooks.
5. Trails—North Carolina—Durham Metropolitan Area—Guidebooks.
6. Trails—North Carolina—Chapel Hill Metropolitan Area—Guidebooks.
7. Raleigh Metropolitan Area (N.C.)—Guidebooks. 8. Durham Metropolitan
Area (N.C.)—Guidebooks. 9. Chapel Hill Metropolitan Area (N.C.)—
Guidebooks. I. Title.
GV199.42.N662R354  1997
796.51'09756'55—dc21          96-39789

*To* *trail researchers, designers, construction*
*workers, maintainers and members of*
*Triangle trail organizations*

# CONTENTS

# ACKNOWLEDGMENTS

While researching and hiking new trails (and many older trails that had changes and relocations) for the third edition of *North Carolina Hiking Trails*, I noticed early in the project the increase in urban trails. Some of my associate writers suggested I divide the research into two guidebooks, one for the state's urban and greenway trails, the other for all remaining types of trails. But after discussions with publishers and outdoor recreation planners, I decided to continue the comprehensive guidebook of nearly 950 trails, then emphasize all trails in large metropolitan areas such as the Triangle and the Triad in separate books. Although this would lead to some duplication, it would add new trails, expand description of some others, and consolidate all the area trails within about 50 or 60 miles.

Beth Timson, regional trail specialist of the North Carolina Division of Parks and Recreation, provided support and inspiration for this project. She was early at the scene when new trails such as those at Leigh Farm in Orange County and Fox Creek Nature Lab in Franklin County were being developed. Additionally, she compiled a valuable list of names, addresses, and telephone numbers for a *Directory of Trail Associations and Trail Managing Agencies in North Carolina*.

Outstanding assistance was provided by resource manager Judson Edeburn, staff specialist Tatjana Vujic, and other staff members of Duke Forest. I am grateful for their time and benevolent sharing of information on history, services, and forest road locations. I also wish to thank Scott Harris, forest assistant at Hill Forest of North Carolina State

University. His guidance was essential in a remote forest without road names or numbers.

My thanks go to park and greenway planner Victor Lebsock and design and development administrator Dick Bailey of the Raleigh Parks and Recreation Department. I also thank planner Guillo Rodriguez and staff associates of the Durham Department of Parks and Recreation for information on current and long-range plans for city trails.

To those hikers who worked with me in preparing trail equipment, trip logistics, and shuttle transportation on the longer linear trails, I express my appreciation. Among them are Robert Ballance of Raleigh, a longtime hiking friend on the *Appalachian Trail, Pacific Crest Trail*, and the Grand Canyon trails; naturalist Vivian Weighmar of Chapel Hill; and Jeff Jeffreys of Durham, a faithful hiking partner and logistical assistant. I also owe special thanks to trail leaders Chris Bracknell, Jim Hallsey, Larkin Kirkman, Darrell McBane, and Bill Flournoy, who have hiked with me or served on committees and boards in the Triangle area. In addition, I am grateful for a cadre of assistants: Debra Smith, Jeff Jones, Ryan Blacher, Benjamin Lenhard, Susan Gallen, Jeff Brewer, Linda McKiddy, and Benjamin Luques.

I appreciate the photographic assistance of Bill Russ and Bridget Maupin at the North Carolina Department of Travel and Tourism; Gene Furr, Paul Magann, and Joe Miller of the *News and Observer* of Raleigh; and the Photofinishing Services Division of the Touchberry Group.

My high regard and thanks go to Gordon Hardy, editor and publisher of Appalachian Mountain Club Books in Boston, and Carolyn Sakowski (president) and Steve Kirk (editor) of John F. Blair, Publisher, in Winston-Salem, for arranging and exchanging my research material to make *Trails of the Triangle* possible.

# INTRODUCTION

In 1996, the *Wall Street Journal* predicted that the Triangle would have the fastest-growing employment rate in the Southeast over the next two years and the second-fastest growth nationally. In 1994, *Money* magazine listed the Triangle as the number-one place to live in the United States.

The uplifting predictions and praise were not new to the residents of Raleigh, Durham, Chapel Hill, and their environs. For example, the *Wall Street Journal* and *Money* articles followed a number of rankings in 1993: *Fortune* magazine named the area the number-one place in the nation to do business; *World Trade* magazine named the Raleigh/Durham area one of the 10 best cities for locating an international company; *Money* ranked the Triangle one of the five best places to live in the nation; and *Parade* magazine named Raleigh/Durham one of the best areas for entrepreneurs. *Child* magazine has rated the area as a good place to raise children. In late 1996, Raleigh was the nation's top city for corporate relocations, according to *Outlook Magazine*, and the adjoining city of Cary led the Triangle in business construction.

While residents express pride in these reports of living standards and business health, there are additional factors that make the quality of life so pleasurable in the Triangle. Two factors are the area's recreational facilities and its protection of the natural environment, the focus of *Trails of the Triangle*. Those of us who have lived in the Triangle for a long time may accept our parks, preserves, botanical gardens, forests, and greenways as routine places to visit and enjoy, but visitors and new residents are fast taking notice also—as are others around the nation.

For example, in 1996, the American Hiking Society awarded Raleigh's greenway system the United States of America Hall of Fame Award. These and other honors are not surprises to us. We have known for some time that we have a remarkable place to live, work, and play.

The term *Triangle* was first used to describe Raleigh, Durham, and Chapel Hill in the early 1950s. It had a central meaning of diverse but complementary relationships; economic, cultural, and scientific exchange; and educational benefits. For the latter, there were three major research universities: Duke University in Durham, the University of North Carolina at Chapel Hill, and North Carolina State University in Raleigh. Thus the term *Research Triangle*. Enrollment in the universities provided a surplus of graduates for the local job market in technology, science, medicine, and related disciplines. To prevent many of the outstanding graduates from leaving North Carolina, metropolitan leaders conceived the idea of Research Triangle Park (RTP). The result was the creation of a 7,000-acre tract adjoining southeast Durham (traversed by I-40) and near the west side of Raleigh/Durham International Airport (RDU). By 1959, research companies were moving in; IBM located in Research Triangle Park in 1965. Today, RTP boasts more than 130 research companies and more than 36,000 employees. Visitors will notice that RTP was planned to leave natural green space and wide walkways for walking and jogging. Eight miles of walkways have been constructed on Cornwallis Road, Alexander Drive, NC-54, and Davis Drive. Another 6 miles are planned.

Geometrically, the area is shaped like an obtuse triangle, with Chapel Hill/Carrboro and Durham having adjoining metropolitan boundaries. Cary, which has a population of more than 70,000 and for the past few years has been the state's fastest-growing city, adjoins Raleigh on the southwest. If Cary is considered part of the Triangle, the shape is more like that of a parallelogram. Together, these four cities have a resident population of more than half a million. Additionally, there is an estimated population of 68,500 college and university students residing in the Triangle area.

Since the early 1990s, the term *Triangle* has grown to represent more than just the three major university cities. The Triangle area now not only includes Wake, Durham, and Orange Counties but the adjoining counties of Chatham, Franklin, and Johnson as well. It is from these six counties that a population of a million was reached in the summer of 1996. The United States Census Bureau revealed that Wake County alone had half that population (517,639), an increase of 20 percent from 1990 to 1995.

In May 1996, the United States Bureau of Economic Analysis predicted that the Triangle would have an increase in population to 1.2 million by 2005. During this period, the Triangle is expected to be the fifth-fastest-growing metropolitan region in the nation. Part of the result will be 196,300 new jobs.

Such growth means an increase in housing, roads, water treatment systems, shopping centers, schools, hospitals, and infrastructure. An example of how Raleigh's citizens are accepting growth was demonstrated in June 1996 when a $250 million school bond was approved by 79 percent of the voters. Growth also means a greater need for parks and recreation. In the summer of 1996, the Durham City Council proposed a $63 million bond issue for infrastructure; $1.5 million would be for improving landscapes and equipment in 35 of the city's 55 parks, most of them in the inner city. The Cary Parks and Recreation Department maintains 13 parks and a number of greenways; others are in the planning stage. Chapel Hill has 14 parks and three greenways, with others on the drawing board.

Raleigh's park planning began in 1974. Its 156 parks and recreation areas have been nationally recognized for their design, management, and service systems. At the time of this writing, the city's award-winning Park and Recreation Department had more than 4,050 acres of land and 1,320 acres of water in its system. A city planner has stated that nearly 50 miles of trails are now complete and another 216 miles are being planned.

This book not only describes the foot trails for day hikes in the metropolitan areas of the Triangle, but also trails in general within a 60-mile radius. This distance easily provides time to visit more than one trail during a day's outing. Backpacking and overnight camping may be planned for a few parks, mainly in the state park system.

## Variety of Trails

The Triangle offers a choice of over 200 trails. Diverse in length and emphasis, they may be limited to foot travel only or may be shared by pedestrians, bikers, and equestrians. Some trails allow in-line skaters. A number of trails are specifically designed for use by the physically impaired; an excellent example is *Big Lake Handicapped Trail* in William B.

Umstead State Park. The trails range from short hikes such as the 0.2-mile *Lassiter's Mill Trail* to the area's longest hike, the 23.4-mile *Falls Lake Trail*, part of *Mountains-to-Sea Trail*. Some trails are interpretive; examples are *Woodland Nature Trail* at Sandling Beach near Falls Lake and *Shepherd Nature Trail* in Duke Forest. The trails in the Triangle range from natural earth and duff to gravel and sand to cement and asphalt—or combinations. On residential trails such as *Shelley Lake Trail*, you may see saunterers, walkers, joggers, runners, bikers, in-line skaters, and pushers of baby strollers; the trail is so popular that there is a speed limit of 10 miles per hour, and a centerline separates traffic. On remote countryside hikes such as *Buckhorn Trail*, you may not see anyone except the Boy Scouts who maintain the trail.

Some trails are in the planning or construction stages. One is *New Hope Overlook Trail* in the New Hope Overlook State Recreation Area of Jordan Lake. Another is *American Tobacco Trail*, a proposed long north-south multiuse route on a former railroad from downtown Durham to NC-751 about 3 miles north of US-1. (Call 919-846-9991 or 919-493-6394 for more information.) A network of equestrian trials is planned on state property east of NC-50 and north of Falls Lake in Wake County. Trails are also being developed in the New Hope Creek corridor managed by the Triangle Land Conservancy; see its address and telephone number in appendix 1.

In September 1996, Hurricane Fran severely damaged some trails in the Triangle. If hiking within a year of Fran's passage through the area, readers may wish to call the park and forest offices to determine trail conditions.

## Maps

Although the maps in this guidebook may prove helpful, it is essential that you have a state and a city map if you are unfamiliar with the area. Free state maps are available at interstate welcome centers, chambers of commerce, some state and city park offices, and the Highway Map Office (Department of Transportation, 1 South Wilmington Street, Raleigh, NC 27601, 919-733-7600). Available for purchase at bookstores and most convenience stores is Delorme's detailed *North Carolina Atlas and Gazetteer*. Detailed city maps include ADC of Alexandria, Inc.'s,

*Durham and Chapel Hill* and *Raleigh and Vicinity* maps and Gousha Travel Publications' city maps. County maps can be helpful for rural and isolated areas; these are sold by the Highway Map Office, chambers of commerce, and county register of deeds offices. *North Carolina County Maps*, which contains maps of all the state's counties in atlas form, is available at some bookstores.

## Health and Pleasure

Walking is our most natural exercise, a historical, biological, and cultural asset. Henry David Thoreau, considered one of America's greatest walkers, said he walked for both health and pleasure. Walking for exercise and mental strength was also part of the philosophy of life among such people as John Ruskin, William Wordsworth, Jane Austen, Thomas Jefferson, Abraham Lincoln, Harry Truman, Emma Gatewood, and coast-to-coast Robert Sweetgall. A more recent figure of note is Warren Doyle, who in 1995 completed the Appalachian Trail for the 10th time, a world record.

*Walking* magazine reported in a 1995 survey of "Why Americans Walk" that 80 percent walk to enjoy the natural scenery, 75 percent for exercise and health, 40 percent for errands, and 17 percent for commuting to work or school. For urbanites, even a walk on the sidewalk is good for health and pleasure. This continues to figure into the design of some sidewalks in Research Triangle Park. Sidewalks can provide a nature walk for viewing birds, squirrels, flowers, trees, streams, and lakes. In some cities, there are historic districts where sidewalks and nature paths are combined. The networking of greenways, a product of the 1980s, is enhancing walking options.

Health specialists say that simple exposure to sunlight on a sidewalk or nature trail can assist in beating the wintertime blues or cabin fever. Health therapist Paula Alder claims that we can "walk out" our problems. A walking habit helps in staying active, shaving off calories, and "dealing more positively with issues." On urban greenways, walkers are likely to see a high percentage of pedestrians walking fast, running, or jogging to lose weight. In 1991, the Weight Control Information Network reported that 31 percent of American adults were overweight, a 10 percent increase from 1962. Despite the benefits of modern medicine, we cannot abandon our need for a healthy diet and plenty of exercise. The most natural and inexpensive method for beginning to acquire and maintain physical and mental health is to take a walk every day. One of the purposes of this book is to emphasize how close you are to walks on alluring and inspiring nature trails in the Triangle area.

## Planning Your Nature Walks

### Who Is Going?

Judgments of where to go and what to take can usually be made quickly by experienced hikers. Beginners may need some assistance from experienced hikers, sports specialists, scoutmasters, or outdoor sports coaches. Outdoor sports associated with walking include backpacking, camping, canoeing, and fishing; the latter may require a license. Some parks offer fields for baseball, football, and soccer, courts for basketball and tennis, and beaches for swimming. With such a variety of options available, you will need advance planning on what gear you will take and what size vehicle you will need. Even with the use of this book, you may have additional questions about the services or schedules at the parks. It is likely that the parks will have brochures or signs to assist in your decisions after your arrival. For parents taking their children on trails and picnic outings, part of the planning may involve choosing a park with playgrounds or a nature museum. If taking senior citizens or those who need wheelchairs, check appendix 2 for suggested trail choices. This book also identifies parks that have boat, bike, or horse rentals. A few parks have nature tour guides.

### Are Your Feet Ready?

A vital part of your plans for walking or hiking should be to have proper footwear. A study made by the American Podiatric Medical Association in 1996 revealed that about 62 percent of Americans assume that it is normal for their feet to hurt, and that about 80 percent endure some type of foot pain regularly. Yet hardly 3 percent visit a podiatrist to determine the cause. A large percentage of people buy shoes from salespeople who are not trained in recommending the best shoes for their customers. A frequent comment is that after you "break them in," shoes will be comfortable. If the shoes are of poor quality, do not have proper toe-box space or arch support, or are in need of custom foot beds and cushioning, you are likely to have discomfort or damage your feet. When replacing good shoes, take the pair with you to a qualified salesperson to assist in the choice of your new shoes. Usually, one foot is larger than the other. The thickness of socks is also an important factor in proper fitting.

If you are a walker, runner, and backpacker, you will need different shoes for each activity. Walking shoes do not need as much heel cushion as running shoes. For most walkers, the heel buildup of running shoes can cause shin muscles to be strained or pulled. When buying backpacking boots, you may wish to examine the "Gear Guide" edition of *Backpacker* magazine or discuss your wishes with a specialist at an outdoor supply store. Dave Getchell, equipment editor of *Backpacker*, says buying hiking boots is like a search for love. In either search, impulsiveness can cause trouble, but a careful match can form a bond for many years. When being fitted, ask the salesperson to use a Brannock measuring device.

For foot maintenance, wear two pairs of socks (one wool or synthetic and one lightweight liner acrylic); wear ankle-high gaiters to prevent skin erosion; protect sore spots with moleskin; wash and dry your feet daily on long trips (there are about a quarter-million pores in the sweat glands); and use foot powder occasionally.

Where in the Triangle will you need hiking boots? In William B. Umstead State Park, parts of Duke Forest's gated roads, *Falls Lake Trail*, North Carolina State University Forest's gated roads, Lake Crabtree County Park, and *Buckhorn Trail*, among other places.

## Trail Clothes

Colin Fletcher wrote in *The Complete Walker III* that the best trail clothes are none at all. In his long hike through the Grand Canyon, he lived by that principle, wearing only boots to protect him against rattlesnakes and a big hat for shade. With all respect to one of America's most authoritative writers on walking, his fashions are not appropriate for the Triangle trails. Instead, hikers should first consult the weather forecast and wear what is comfortable. Walkers can settle the most serious matter of dress when they pamper their feet with perfect shoes. Clothes should keep you warm and dry, in thermal equilibrium. If it is cool and you are sweating due to fast walking, jogging, or running, you may need both an absorbent garment and a Gore-Tex shell. Whatever you choose, be aware of the risk of hypothermia when cooling down too rapidly.

Long-sleeve shirts and trousers are recommended for brushy trails in such places as Jordan and Falls Lakes, where ticks and other biting bugs can easily get on your skin. Some experts also recommend light-colored clothing. If you are hiking on game lands or hunting preserves during hunting season, you must wear an orange-blazed jacket and cap. If backpacking on long or overnight trails in the Triangle, choose extra clothing appropriate for the season. Local trail-supply stores have an outstanding diversity of trail clothes and gear and can provide counsel on what is best for your excursions.

The Triangle's climate is moderate, with seasonal averages of 41 degrees in winter, 60 degrees in spring, 78 degrees in summer, and 60 degrees in autumn. It rains an average of 112 days during the year.

## What's in Your Daypack?

A daypack (waist or shoulders) is desirable when you will be on a trail long enough to need water, food, rainwear, or first aid. Some trail consultants insist that you should take a daypack if you are going to be out of sight of your home or vehicle. Among the basics items you will need are maps, water, nutritional food, a first-aid kit, a pocketknife, insect repellant, a flashlight, a whistle or other alarm, a handkerchief, spare clothing, a rain jacket with a hood, notepaper, and pens. You should also carry FastAid, a small, folding, cardlike first-aid guide that provides instructions for dealing with 31 potential emergencies; there is a place on the guide to include emergency telephone numbers for ambulance, rescue squad, personal doctor, hospital, and family members. If you are on a nature outing, you may need a camera and binoculars—how often have you caught yourself saying, "If only I'd taken my camera"? Children—particularly those between the ages of nine and 15—usually like to be outdoors regardless of whether they are hiking, playing games, or exploring. They will enjoy the trails even more if accompanied by siblings or friends in the same age group. Make a daypack for each of them. And finally, if the family dog is large enough, provide it with a "dogpack" for its food and water.

## Trail Security

The trails in this book are unlighted and do not have designated police patrols except at parking areas in urban locations during the night. Only a few trails have emergency telephones, *Duke Cross Country Trail* and *Black Creek Trail* among them.

The first rule of security is not to hike the trails after dark. Many of the signs at the trailheads specifically state that the trails are closed after dusk. Other suggestions for security are to lock your vehicle and to not leave valuable items where they can be seen through the windows; to inform someone in your family or a friend where you are going and when you expect to return; to always keep your eyes and ears alert (headsets with loud music may interfere with the sounds of impending danger); to take a cellular telephone with you; and, of course, to have one or more partners with you whenever possible. Walking on a wide, scenic greenway, seeing so many happy faces, hearing laughter from children playing, and sharing friendly greetings with strangers may make you wonder how anything could go wrong. But it has in the past and will again. Residents of the Triangle and other urban areas are justified in their concern over the increase in crime.

## Trail Courtesy

Some trail courtesy rules are distinctive to a locality, some are written on signs in parks and subdivision greenways, and others are generally accepted but unwritten. On multiuse trails, the first rule is to share space, much as on sidewalks or streets. Pedestrians have the right of way unless otherwise posted. Signs indicating that some trails are for foot travel only should be respected. Pets must be kept on a leash and prevented from soiling treadways and playgrounds. Avoid leaving trash on the trails, damaging plants, harassing wildlife, and playing boom boxes at offending volumes.

How friendly you are to strangers depends on your personality and the reasons for the conversation. Taking photos or serving as a tour guide is an automatic icebreaker. If I am on a new trail or rehiking a relocated trail, my measuring wheel is frequently an introductory subject. Children are the most likely to ask, "What is that thing?" or "Is that a unicycle?" Adults may stare but feel it impolite to ask. One adult stranger in Eno River State Park stopped and stared; after my explanation, he chuckled and suggested I get something I could ride. A long and friendly conversation followed.

Welcome to the trails of the Triangle.

# LEGEND FOR MAPS

| | |
|---|---|
| 🚶 · · · · · · · · · · · | Hiking Trail |
| 🚲 🏇 – – – – – | Bicycling, Equestrian, or General |
| ▦▦▦⊗▦▦▦ | Railroad |
| **P** | Parking Lot |
| **?** | Information |
| Phone | Telephone |
| 🛆 | Picnic Table |
| 🏚 | Picnic Shelter |
| 🚹🚺 | Restroom |
| ⛺ | Camping |
| 🐟 | Fishing |
| 🏊 | Swimming |
| 🚿 | Shower |
| ♿ | Wheelchair Accessible |

# TRAILS OF THE TRIANGLE

*Spider-rooted sycamore on Woodland Nature Trail,
Sandling Beach State Recreation Area, Falls Lake*

# Chapter 1

## TRAILS ON UNITED STATES GOVERNMENT PROPERTIES

━━━━━━━━━━━━━━━━━━━

Formed during the early years of the nation as part of the Continental Army, the United States Army Corps of Engineers had its beginning at West Point, a garrison on the Hudson River. In 1798, the Corps was enlarged, and in 1802 Congress made West Point a military academy. Since then, Congress has authorized a wide range of Corps projects. Among them have been blazing and building roads, clearing waterways and harbors, building dams for flood control and hydroelectric power, protecting and restoring shorelines, providing natural-disaster relief, ensuring fish and wildlife development, and enhancing recreational opportunities. While emphasizing diversity in recreational usage, the Corps enforces zoning regulations to protect the ecology.

There are four major Corps projects in North Carolina: B. Everett Jordan Dam and Lake (Haw and New Hope Rivers), Falls Lake (Neuse River), John H. Kerr Dam and Reservoir (Staunton/Roanoke and Dan Rivers), and W. Kerr Scott Dam and Reservoir (Yadkin River). All were constructed for the major purpose of preventing downstream flood damage. With the exception of the Scott project, acreage is leased by the state's Department of Environment, Health, and Natural Resources (DEHNR) for recreational purposes and is managed by the Division of Parks and Recreation. These properties are described by the DEHNR as state recreation areas (SRAs). The Corps also leases acreage to the state's

Wildlife Resources Commission for wildlife management and motorboat registration on all four projects. Examples of other types of leases are Wilkes County Park at the Scott project and Blue Jay Point County Park at the Falls Lake project and commercial leases such as marinas on all the projects (usually subleased by the DEHNR). Another example is Penny's Bend Nature Preserve, managed by the North Carolina Botanical Garden. All the projects have trails.

For information, contact Division of Wildlife Management, 512 North Salisbury Street, Raleigh, NC 27604-1188 (919-733-7291).

## B. EVERETT JORDAN DAM AND LAKE

### Chatham, Durham, Orange, and Wake Counties

The United States Congress instructed the Corps of Engineers to study the historic Cape Fear River basin in 1945 for flood control. A lake, known then as New Hope Lake, was authorized in 1963 and constructed in 1967. In 1973, it was renamed in honor of United States senator B. Everett Jordan. Since then, the North Carolina Division of Parks and Recreation has managed nearly 14,000 acres of the 46,768-acre project as SRAs. Twelve areas are now developed, some of which have trails. The most popular recreational activities are boating, fishing, water-skiing, sailing, windsurfing, camping, and swimming.

The SRAs without named or completed trails are as follows.

New Hope Overlook SRA is scheduled to have the 5-mile *New Hope Overlook Trail* completed in 1997. The park also offers a boat ramp, fishing, and hike-in tent camping. Access is off US-1 on SR-1700 northwest of the Haw River bridge.

Roberson SRA offers a boat ramp and fishing.

Crosswinds Boat Ramp SRA offers a boat ramp, restrooms, a telephone, and fishing.

Poplar Point Campground SRA offers tent and RV camping, with a ramp and a swimming beach for campers only. Its campsites connect with unnamed foot trails.

Crosswinds Campground SRA offers tent and RV camping, with a boat ramp and a swimming beach for campers only. Unnamed connecting trails run between the boat ramp and campgrounds A, B, and C.

*B. Everett Jordan Dam and Lake*
*Photo courtesy of North Carolina Travel and Tourism*

Parkers Creek SRA has tent, RV, and group tent camping, with a pic-nic area and a boat ramp for campers only. It also offers fishing and a public swimming area. There is a short children's trail around picnic shelter #3.

The three SRAs described below have specifically named foot trails. As facilities continue to develop, visitors are requested to call in ad-vance for an update on services.

*Address and Access:* Superintendent, Jordan Lake SRA, Route 2, Box 159, Apex, NC 27502 (919-362-0586). Access is off US-64 South via the last road before crossing the causeway/bridge 3.7 miles west of the US-64/NC-751 junction.

Currently, approximately 18,000 acres of the Jordan Lake prop-erty are managed by the North Carolina Wildlife Resources Com-mission. One of the outstanding areas for nature study is the

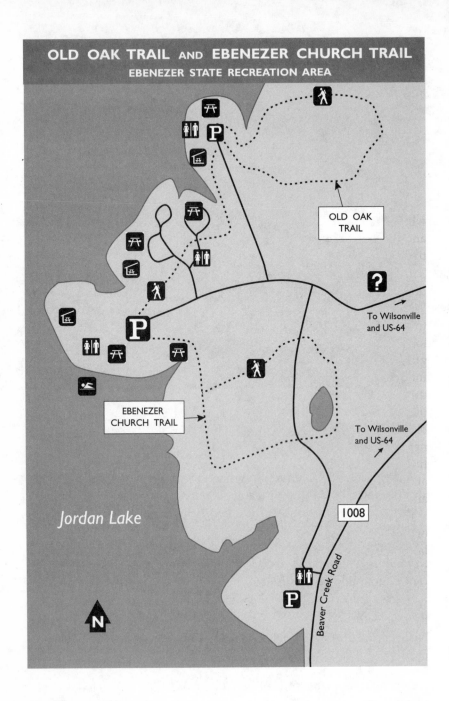

OLD OAK TRAIL AND EBENEZER CHURCH TRAIL
EBENEZER STATE RECREATION AREA

OLD OAK TRAIL

To Wilsonville
and US-64

EBENEZER
CHURCH TRAIL

To Wilsonville
and US-64

Jordan Lake

1008

Beaver Creek Road

N

commission's Wildlife Observation Deck. In the summertime, bald eagles may be seen from the observation deck, usually early in the morning or late in the day. Access to the observation site is via a narrow road (which has a sign) leading west off NC-751. (NC-751 is 6.1 miles south of I-40, exit 274, or 5.6 miles north of US-64.) From the parking lot, you can enter a gated area on *Wildlife Observation Trail,* a birder's delight. After 0.1 mile, you will begin a 1.4-mile loop. The right turn leads 0.6 mile to the observation deck. On the approach is a patch of blackberry, usually ripe the last week of June. The more remote part of the trail leads over former tobacco fields and into damp areas near the lake, where other wildlife and plant life may be observed. Call the Recreation Management Center at 919-362-0586 for information on interpretive bird-watching tours. (USGS map: Green Level)

At Ebenezer Church SRA are two trails for foot traffic only. Access is off US-64 at the junction with Beaver Creek Road (SR-1008) in Wilsonville; drive south for 2.1 miles and turn right. Take the first road to the right after the entrance and park on the east side of the parking lot at a trail sign. Hike the easy, red-blazed *Old Oak Trail* past a bamboo grove at a sign about diving ducks at 0.4 mile. Complete a loop of 0.9 mile through a pine forest and tall oak. Return to the entrance road, drive right, and park at the nearest access to the lake on the left at a picnic area; you will see a sign for Ebenezer Church. Follow the red-blazed *Ebenezer Church Trail* (for foot traffic only) on an old road. After nearly 0.2 mile, the former site of the historic church is to the right, but turn left off the road. Walk through a young forest, cross a paved road at 0.4 mile, curve around a tranquil small pond, cross the road again, and return to the parking area at 1 mile. (USGS map: New Hope Dam)

At Seaforth SRA is the 1.6-mi *Pond Trail,* for foot traffic only. (Map is on next page.) Access is off US-64 via the first left after crossing the lake's causeway/bridge west from Wilsonville. Park near the end of the parking area across from the beach bathhouse and enter the red-blazed trail through an oak forest mixed with loblolly pine. At 0.2 mile, you will cross a boardwalk for an exceptionally beautiful view of the lake. By the boardwalk are lizard's tail, marsh mallow, and fragrant buttonbush. You will circle left of a pond with a beaver hutch at 0.6 mile, then pass through a field of lespedeza, cross the entrance road, walk through a loblolly pine forest, pass a former pond site with willow, and exit at a picnic shelter. Cross the parking area for a return to the point of origin.

On your return to US-64, drive west for 2.5 miles to Griffins Crossroad

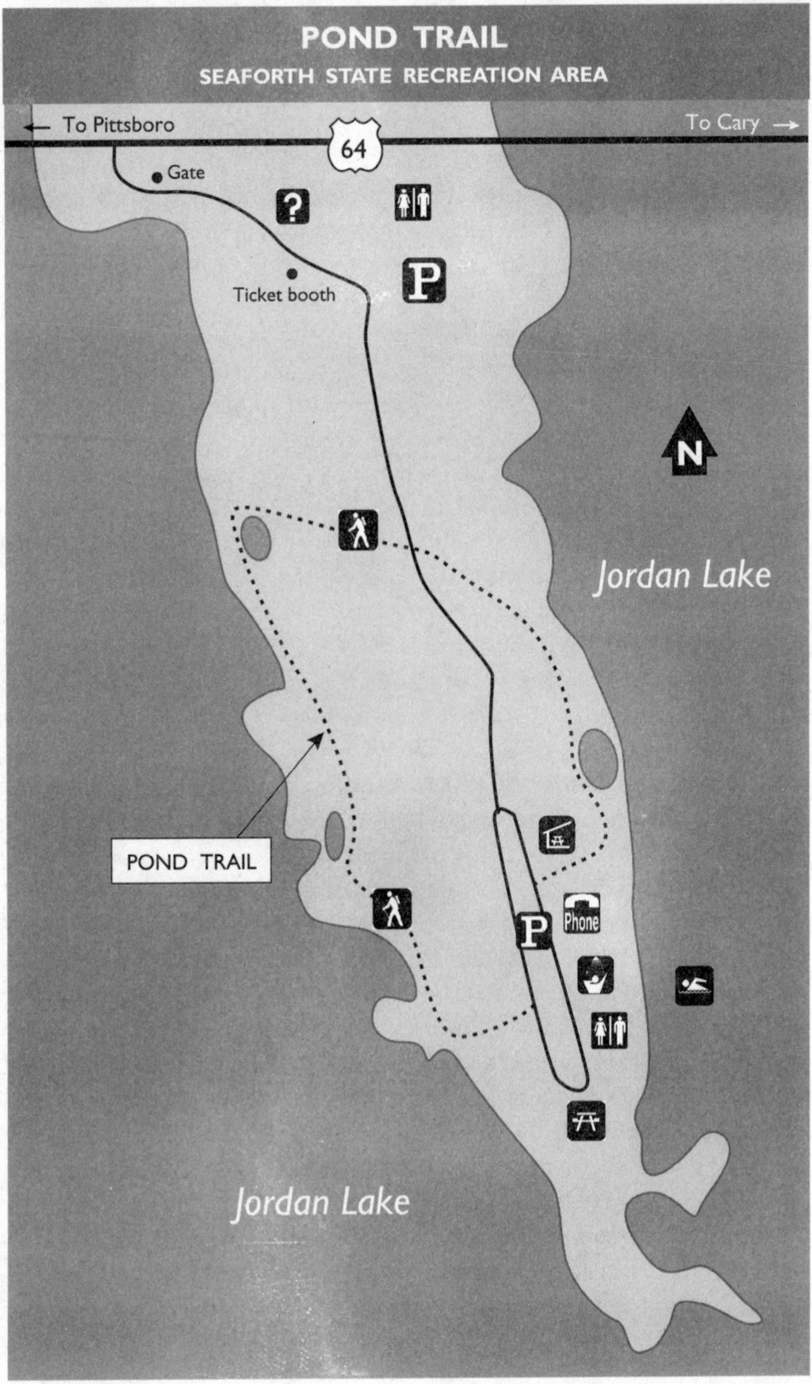
POND TRAIL
SEAFORTH STATE RECREATION AREA
To Pittsboro
64
To Cary
Gate
Ticket booth
N
Jordan Lake
POND TRAIL
Phone
Jordan Lake

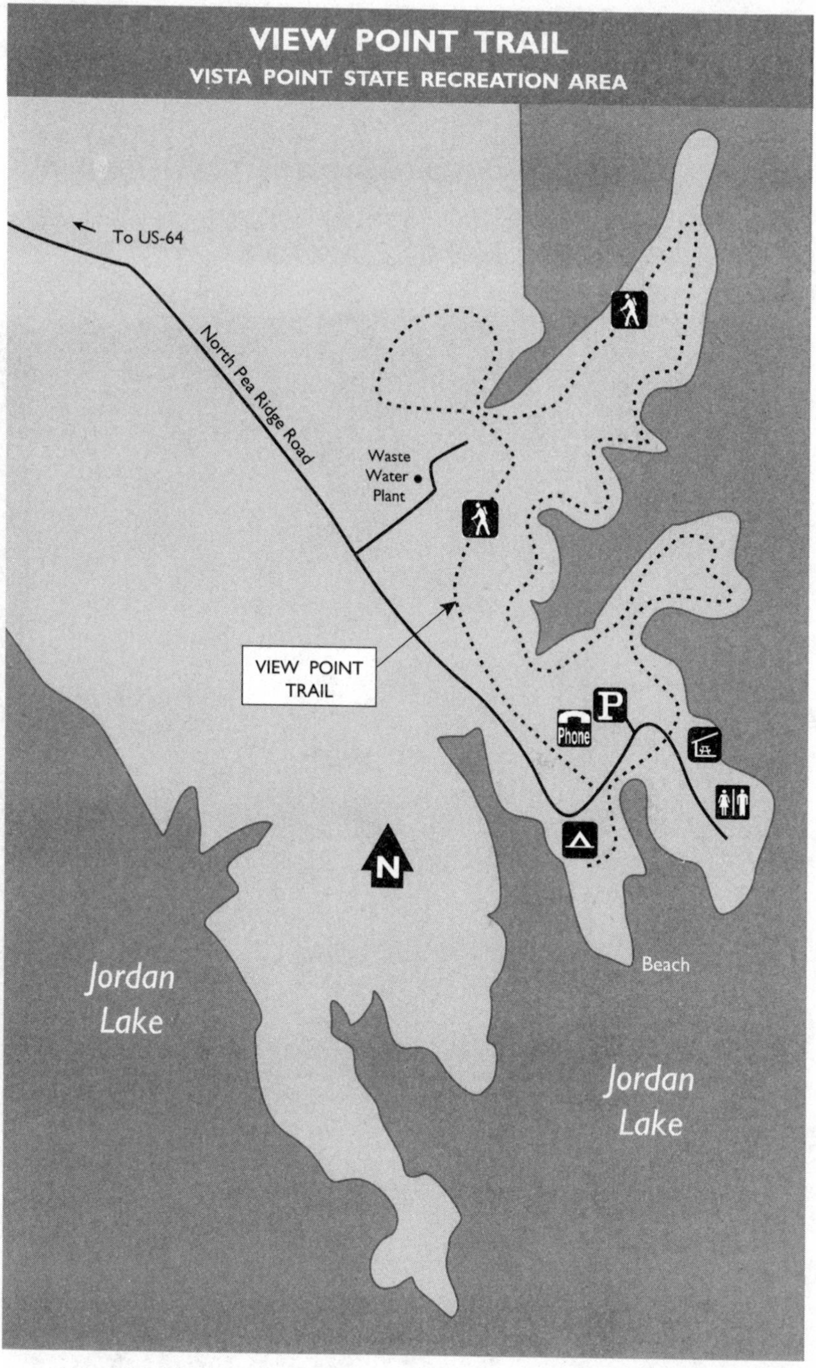

# VIEW POINT TRAIL
## VISTA POINT STATE RECREATION AREA

To US-64

North Pea Ridge Road

Waste
Water
Plant

VIEW POINT
TRAIL

Phone

P

N

Beach

Jordan
Lake

Jordan
Lake

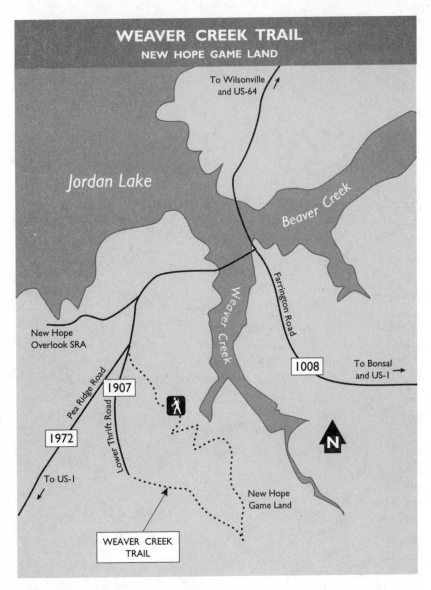

# WEAVER CREEK TRAIL
## NEW HOPE GAME LAND

To Wilsonville
and US-64

Jordan Lake

Beaver Creek

Weaver Creek

Farrington Road

New Hope
Overlook SRA

Pea Ridge Road

Lower Thrift Road

1907

1972

1008

To Bonsal
and US-1

To US-1

N

New Hope
Game Land

WEAVER CREEK
TRAIL

(located 5 miles east of Pittsboro) and turn left (south) on Pea Ridge Road (SR-1700) to Vista Point SRA. After 2.5 miles, park on the left before the entrance booth. Begin the red-blazed, 2.7-mile *View Point Trail* (for foot traffic only) through a mixed forest of oak, maple, and pine. (Map is on page 9.) At 0.7 mile is a proposed loop extension. At 0.8 mile is a lake view to the left. At 1.1 miles is evidence of former tobacco rows. For the next 1.2 miles, you will curve in and out of a series of coves, sometimes passing close enough to view the lake through the trees. Footbridges cross the ravines. Forest growth remains the same, with occasional holly, sparkleberry, and fern beds. You will pass left of a group RV campground at 2.3 miles and right of a picnic shelter at 2.5 miles. You will then cross a paved road and junction with a blue-blazed trail, located to the left at 2.6 miles. (This is a walk-in route to campsites which continues to an old barn and wellhouse.) Keep right and exit to the parking area where the trail began.

The 3.8-mile *Weaver Creek Trail* (2.2 miles one-way in the forest) is a project of the Chatham County Task Force and the Triangle Greenways Council. To reach the trailhead, drive south on SR-1008 from the junction of US-64 and SR-1008 at Wilsonville, cross a bridge over Jordan Lake, and at 3.7 miles turn right on Pea Ridge Road (SR-1972). Cross Weaver Creek Cove and at 1.1 miles turn left at Lower Thrift Road (SR-1907). Park on the left in the flat, grassy area. The trail sign has a hikers' symbol and yellow-dot blaze. If hiking the trail during hunting season, wear an orange-blazed jacket and cap. The seasons begin with dove and quail around September 1 and last through deer season to February 28. Call 800-662-7350 for information.

The trail enters a forest of loblolly pine and hardwoods with an understory of sourwood, dogwood, and holly. Patches of Christmas fern and club moss are along the way. There are five short footbridges. The trail is gentle; ridge elevations feather out to Weaver Creek Cove. Wildlife is prominent, particularly deer and squirrel. The area also offers a variety of habitats for birds. In the warm season, black snake and hognose snake may be seen. The hognose snake (*Heterodon platyrhinos*), also called puff adder, is likely to alert you to its presence by hissing and spreading its head in the shape of a cobra.

You will cross an intermittent stream at 0.4 mile. At 1.1 miles is a view of the lake to the left in the wintertime. Sensitive fern is located near a number of damp areas. At 1.8 miles are the last stream crossing and wooden bridge. You will exit the forest at 2.2 miles into a grassy saddle dam. Turn right and arrive at a gate at 2.8 miles. After a short passage through pines, you will exit at the dead end of Lower Thrift Road. (A private residence has a sign indicating that no parking is permitted at this area.) Follow the gravel road for a return to the trailhead at 3.8 miles. (USGS map: New Hope Dam)

*View of Falls Lake from Falls Lake Trail*

12 TRAILS OF THE TRIANGLE

# FALLS LAKE

Durham, Granville, and Wake Counties

The Falls Lake project encompasses 38,886 acres (11,620 of water and 27,266 of land). Falls Lake received its name from the Falls of the Neuse, a short section of rapids below the dam. The project has 12 public-use sites, seven of which are SRAs managed by the Division of Parks and Recreation: Beaver Dam, B. W. Wells, Highway 50, Holly Point, Sandling Beach, Shinleaf, and Rolling View. Boating, water-skiing, sailing, fishing, and picnicking are the major activities. Hiking the 23.4-mile *Falls Lake Trail*, described below, is another significant recreational activity. The trail is being constructed on the southern boundary of the lake as a joint project of the Division of Parks and Recreation, the Triangle Greenways Council, and the Corps of Engineers. A continuation of the trail from NC-50 to other recreational areas along the Corps property has been proposed through areas of the N.C. Wildlife Resources Commission.

Beaver Dam SRA offers boat access, beach swimming, fishing, and picnic shelters.

B. W. Wells SRA has a campground for RV, tent, and group camping for registered campers only. About 3 miles of trails are planned to connect the campgrounds. B. W. Wells Rock Cliff Farm is here also but is closed to vehicular traffic. The historic farm has a network of short forest and wildflower nature trails that connect to an interpretive center. The four loops are *Ziegles Trail* (1.0 mile), *Terrace Trail* (0.6 mile), *Holly Trail* (0.6 mile), and *Moonshine Trail* (0.8 mile). For information and tour arrangements, contact Benson Kirkman of B. W. Wells Association, Inc., at 919-859-1187.

Highway 50 SRA offers a boat launch, picnic shelters, and fishing.

Holly Point SRA offers beach swimming, a boat ramp, fishing, and a full-service campground for registered campers only.

Sandling Beach SRA offers a beach for swimmers, a boat launch/boat beach, fishing, picnic shelters, and about 2 miles of unnamed foot trails between the picnic shelters and the beach. Across the road from the parking lot of picnic shelter #1 is *Woodland Nature Trail*. (See map on page 14.) The trail is a 24-station, 0.7-mile interpretive loop through a mixed hardwood forest of pine, cedar, oak, beech, sycamore, maple, poplar, and hornbeam. Ferns and running cedar (club moss) are part of the ground cover. After descending, the trail goes upstream among tall

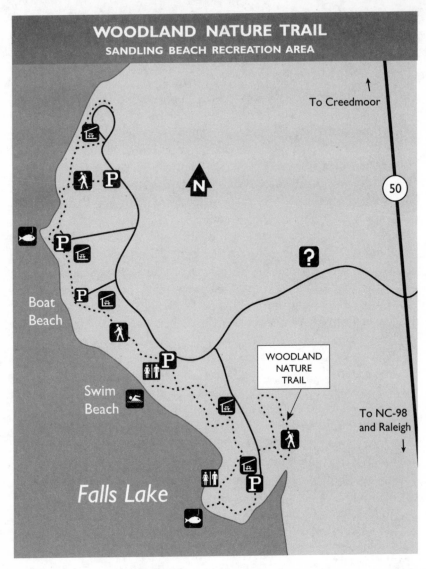

## WOODLAND NATURE TRAIL
### SANDLING BEACH RECREATION AREA

To Creedmoor

**N**

50

Boat
Beach

WOODLAND
NATURE
TRAIL

Swim
Beach

To NC-98
and Raleigh

Falls Lake

trees. At 0.3 mile are a sycamore and a maple with pyramid-shaped roots, the most unique feature of the trail. The trail ascends to a slight ridge for a return to the point of origin. From NC-50, access is 2.2 miles north of the management office of Falls Lake SRA and 5.5 miles south of Creedmoor.

Shinleaf SRA is a hike-in primitive area for camping only; see section 3 of *Falls Lake Trail* on page 20.

Rolling View SRA (see map on page 16) offers a boat ramp, beach swimming, campgrounds (RV, group, and tent, with electrical hookups and hot showers), a community building, fishing, a marina, picnic shelters, and 3.2 miles (including some backtracking) of well-designed, white-blazed, unnamed connecting trails to the beaches, the picnic shelters, the campground, and the community building. From the parking lot for the swimming beach, the trails offer a 1.7-mile round-trip hike in an oak and pine forest to the family campground and a 1.5-mile round-trip hike, also in an oak and pine forest, to the group campground and the community building. On a connector trail between loops A and B in the family campground is a scenic spot with a small waterfall and pool under an overhanging rock. Buckeye and saxifrage grow on the stream banks.

*Address and Access:* Falls Lake SRA Management Office, 13304 Creedmoor Road, Wake Forest, NC 27587 (919-676-1027). From the junction of NC-98 and NC-50, drive north on NC-50 for 1.6 miles; access is to the right. The address for the Corps of Engineers Resources Manager's Office is 11405 Falls of the Neuse Road, Wake Forest, NC 27587 (919-846-9332). Access is 0.9 mile south from the Falls Lake parking area below the dam.

## Falls Lake Trail
### Section 1   Falls of the Neuse to Six Forks Road

*Length and Difficulty:* 13.2 miles, moderate

*Trailhead and Description:* This well-designed and well-maintained trail section was designated a state trail as part of *Mountains-to-Sea Trail* (*MST*) on April 11, 1987. It passes through a hardwood forest, weaves in and out of coves, crosses numerous small drainages, ascends to a number of gentle ridges, and offers occasional scenic views of the lake. The mature forest has a few old-growth trees and some specific evidence of succession. For example, a few places have young growth among former tobacco rows. Holly, laurel, loblolly pine, Christmas fern, wild ginger, and running cedar comprise the winter greenery. Among the ferns are royal, cinnamon, sensitive, resurrection, ebony, southern lady, and bracken. Wildflowers include three species of wild orchid, coral bell, squirrel cup (*Hepatica americana*), mandrake, yellow root, and spring beauty (*Claytonia virginica*). Some of the more evident mammals are deer, beaver, fox, squirrel, and raccoon.

Access to the eastern trailhead is at the Tailwater Fishing Access

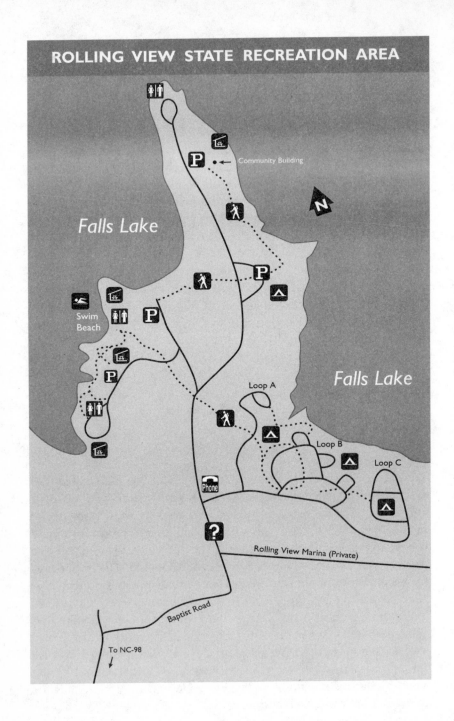

ROLLING VIEW STATE RECREATION AREA

Falls Lake

← Community Building

P

P

Falls Lake

Swim Beach

P

P

Loop A

Loop B

Loop C

Phone

?

Rolling View Marina (Private)

Baptist Road

To NC-98

N

Area parking lot, located below the dam on Falls of the Neuse Road (SR-2000) in North Raleigh. To access the trailhead from the junction of US-1 and NC-98 at Wake Forest, drive 0.7 mile west on NC-98 to Old US-98, turn left, then follow the signs 2.4 miles to the parking area. (Other access points will be described along the trail route.) The trailhead may not have signs or blazes; it is located in front of the restrooms at a two-car parking space. (Do not go up the path to the dam.)

Follow an old service road where white blazes line the route. You will pass through loblolly pine, sweet gum, tulip poplar, and oak with an understory of holly and dogwood. At 0.1 mile, turn left on a foot trail. After 110 yards, the trail forks near a unique double tulip poplar. Take either route. (The blue-blazed trail, to the left, goes 0.6 mile to rejoin the main trail.) On the main trail, turn right and cross the paved dam road; you will arrive at the parking lot of the Corps' Operational Management Center at 0.3 mile. Follow the lakeside road; after 0.2 mile, you will reenter the forest, which features scattered jessamine and redbud. You will cross a Corps service road and junction with the blue-blazed alternate route at 0.9 mile. Turn right. You will cross a pipeline right of way at 1.5 miles, a scenic stream area at 2 miles, and footbridges over streams at 2.3 miles and 2.6 miles. You will then pass some fine views of the lake between the streams and your arrival at Raven Ridge Road (SR-2002) at 3.4 miles. (If you turn left, it is 3.9 miles on Raven Ridge Road and Falls of the Neuse Road to the eastern trailhead.) Turn right and cross the Honeycutt Creek causeway to reenter the woods, right, at 3.5 miles. You will enter a clear-cut area at 4.4 miles, followed by a series of small stream crossings and an old power-line clearing at the edge of a residential area. At 5 miles, you will pass an old farm pond and farm area, followed by a cove and large beech trees. You will arrive at a residential area and an exit to Possum Track Road at 6.1 miles. (To the right, the road is barricaded, but to the left it offers vehicle access, after 6.2 miles, to the trail's origin; after 1.4 miles, to Raven Ridge Road, left; after 2.9 miles, to Falls of the Neuse Road, left; and after 1.9 miles, to the parking lot, left.)

Continuing on *Falls Lake Trail*, cross the road into a grove of loblolly pine. You will cross a paved road at 6.4 miles, enter another pine forest grove at 6.6 miles, and pass lake views at 7.7 miles. You will then cross a couple of ravines before crossing a footbridge at 8.5 miles. At 8.8 miles, you will reach an old woods road. Turn right; you will arrive at Possum Track Road at 9 miles. (The junction with Raven Ridge Road is 0.2 mile to the left.) Turn right and cross the Cedar Creek causeway. At 9.2 miles,

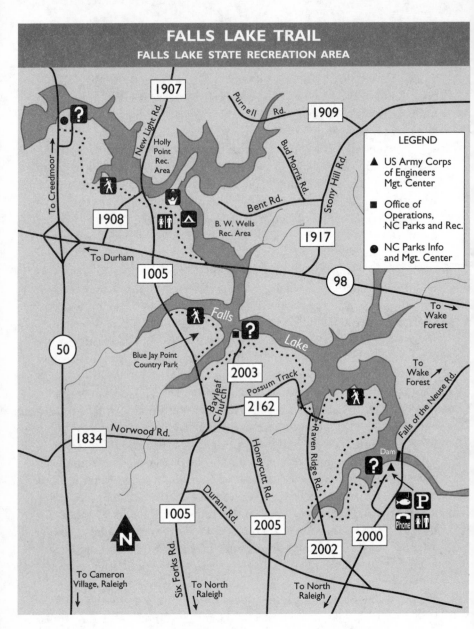

turn right into a pine forest with cedar and honeysuckle. You will pass remnants of an old homestead on the right at 10.1 miles, then enter a scenic area of large beech trees and cross a footbridge at 10.2 miles. After enjoying views of the lake at 10.7 miles, you will enter a section of laurel for the next 0.6 mile. At 12 miles, you will arrive at Bayleaf Church Road (SR-2003). (To the right is the Yorkshire Center of Falls Lake Recreation Area; to the left on the gated road, it is 1 mile to Bayleaf Baptist Church and a junction with Possum Track Road.) Cross the road at the exit sign of the Yorkshire Center and reenter the forest. You will cross a number of small streams in rocky areas and arrive at the end of the guardrail on Six Forks Road (SR-1005) at the Lower Barton Creek causeway at 13.2 miles.

To the right, it is 2.2 miles to NC-98. To the left, it is 7.9 miles back to the parking lot below the dam. The vehicle route is 0.7 mile on Six Forks Road, where a left turn follows Possum Track Road and Raven Ridge Road as described above. (USGS maps: Bayleaf, Wake Forest)

## Section 2   Six Forks Road and Blue Jay Point County Park

*Length and Difficulty:* 3.4 miles, moderate

*Trailhead and Description:* From the trailhead on Six Forks Road (described previously), follow the road to the right (north) across the Lower Barton Creek causeway for 0.3 mile to the end-of-the-road railing at the gravel road-shoulder parking area.

Turn right and enter Blue Jay Point County Park through the forest. You will follow an old woods road for 0.1 mile before descending on a footpath to cross a footbridge. Here are wildflowers and unique roots to a maple tree. You will ascend and descend in and out of coves and cross footbridges. At 0.9 mile are patches of spicebush, wild ginger, and hepatica. At 1.6 miles is the first of four color-coded spur trails you will encounter for the next 0.7 mile. They cross or join *Falls Lake Trail* from the recreational areas on top of the peninsula. *Blue Jay Point Trail* (0.2 mile in length) is the first to cross. *Laurel Trail* (0.2 mile in length) follows. The next trail leads to a trail for the physically disabled. The last trail, *Sandy Point Trail* (0.2 mile in length), originates at the park lodge. There are rock piles left by early farmers at 2 miles. You will come out of the forest at 2.3 miles and reach a display board and a parking lot between a ball field and the park lodge. Cross the paved road and descend to footbridges; follow the undulating trail through hardwoods and loblolly pine to reach Six Forks Road at 3.4 miles at a trail sign. Here is the temporary end of this section.

To the right, it is 1 mile to NC-98. To the left, it is 1.3 miles to the western trailhead of section 1. (USGS map: Bayleaf)

## Section 3   NC-98 to NC-50

*Length and Difficulty:* 6.8 miles, moderate

*Trailhead and Description:* From the intersection of Six Forks Road and NC-98, drive east 1.5 miles on NC-98 to the western edge of the lake bridge. A gravel parking area is on the north side of the road.

At 0.1 mile, you will pass under a power line among redbud, sumac, and blackberry. You will cross a number of footbridges in coves and enter a grove of large beech and tulip poplar at 0.7 mile. The scattered understory contains dogwood, holly, and sparkleberry. You can also enjoy views of the lake here. At 1.1 miles is a scenic area with large beech and wildflowers; at 1.5 miles, near cove waters, is a skillfully designed footbridge. Another scenic lake area features infrequent tawny pine-sap (*Monotropa hypopithus*); also at 2.6 miles is Indian pipe (*Monotropa uniflora*), of the same genus. After a number of footbridges and hilly climbs, you will reach Shinleaf Recreation Area, a walk-in campground with central restrooms and showers, at 3 miles. (To access the recreation area by vehicle, travel 0.5 mile north on New Light Road from the NC-98 junction, located opposite the north end of Six Forks Road.) Cross the parking area and enter the forest; to the left is Norwood Cemetery. You will descend steeply and ascend. At 3.5 miles, exit to New Light Road. (To the left, it is 1.5 miles to NC-98.)

Turn right on New Light Road. After 0.1 mile, turn left up an embankment; watch for the sign, as the turn may be easy to miss. You will enter a low area with large ironwood and spots of yellow root at 3.9 miles, then ascend to cross paved Ghoston Road at 4 miles. You will descend to banks of mayapple, foamflower, and crested dwarf iris and cross the dam of a small pond at 4.6 miles. You will pass around a rocky knoll at 5.1 miles; notice the former tobacco field ridges on the hillside. At 5.3 miles, you will pass to the right of an unnamed cemetery near an old homesite. On an old road of red clay, you will approach a junction with a grassy road at 5.6 miles. Turn left (avoid the grassy road to the extreme left) and exit the road to the right at 5.7 miles. Because of logging, the next two turns (left and right) may require alertness. After the right turn through young pine, you will follow a grassy, open road bordered in sections with orange cow-itch vine. You will cross two paved roads (the latter for the State Management Center, to the right) at 6.6 miles. Exit at the edge of a highway railing on NC-50 at 6.8 miles. There are proposed plans to continue the trail on the south side of the lake to connect with the other trails at Eno River State Park.

To the right, it is 0.1 mile to the gravel road-shoulder parking area. To the left (south), it is 1.6 miles on NC-50 to NC-98. (USGS maps: Bayleaf, Creedmoor)

## JOHN H. KERR DAM AND RESERVOIR

Granville, Vance, and Warren Counties in North Carolina;
Charlotte, Halifax, and Mecklenburg Counties in Virginia

This reservoir of 48,900 acres was completed in 1952 and named for the North Carolina congressman whose leadership made it possible. More than three-fourths of the project's acreage is in Virginia. The reservoir boasts 29 recreation areas. Nine of them are in North Carolina, including 6,200 land acres leased to the state by the Corps. The chief activities in the project are boating, sailing, water-skiing, fishing, swimming, picnicking, and camping. There are 850 numbered campsites among the following parks: Bullocksville, County Line, Hibernia, Henderson Point, Kimball Point, Nutbush Bridge, and Satterwhite Point. All campgrounds open April 1 or Easter (whichever comes first) and close as late as November 1; after that date, all water sources are cut off. Portions of three campgrounds (Cooper Point at Satterwhite, Nutbush Bridge, and Hibernia) are open all year. All campgrounds have sections with electrical and water hookups. Three commercial marinas offer full service for fishermen, boaters, and campers. Among the special events in the parks is the Governor's Cup Invitational Regatta in June. Only the recreation areas with nature trails are covered below. See *The Trails of Virginia: Hiking the Old Dominion* by Allen de Hart for trails on the Virginia side of the reservoir. (USGS maps: Middleburg, Townsville, John H. Kerr Dam, Tungsten)

*Address and Access:* Superintendent, Kerr Reservoir SRA, Route 3, Box 800, Henderson, NC 27536 (919-438-7791). At the I-85 junction in north Henderson, take Satterwhite Road (SR-1319) north for 6 miles.

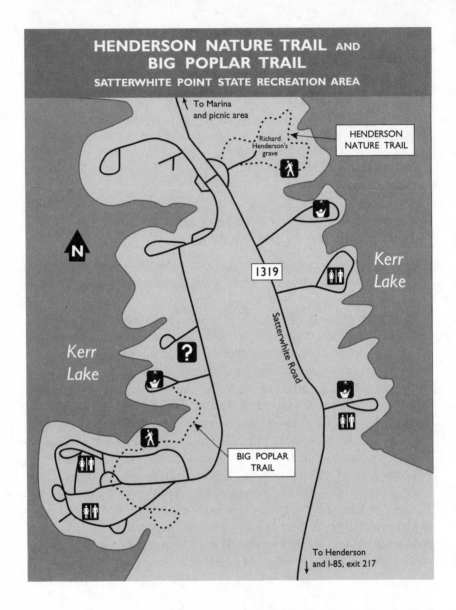

HENDERSON NATURE TRAIL AND
BIG POPLAR TRAIL
SATTERWHITE POINT STATE RECREATION AREA

To Marina
and picnic area

Richard
Henderson's
grave

HENDERSON
NATURE TRAIL

Kerr
Lake

N

1319

Satterwhite Road

Kerr
Lake

?

BIG POPLAR
TRAIL

To Henderson
and I-85, exit 217

The 0.4-mile *Big Poplar Trail* and the 0.6-mile *Henderson Nature Trail* are at Satterwhite Point; the access is described above.

Access to *Big Poplar Trail* is in the J. C. Cooper Campground. This linear trail runs between the wash house (left of the fork at campsite section 105–123) and the entrance loop (right of campsite section 1–15). A wide trail in a mature forest, it could also be called "Big Beech Trail"

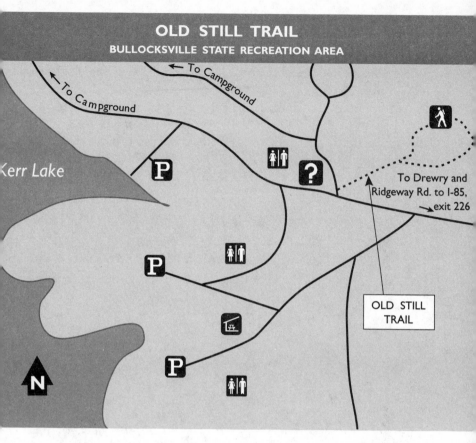

(tree-carving dates are in the late 1800s) or "Big White Oak Trail." A large tulip poplar grows halfway on the trail at a streamlet.

On Satterwhite Road across from the J. C. Cooper Campground entrance is the entrance to *Henderson Nature Trail*. This trail loops from the Henderson kiosk at the Outdoor Lab of the Vance Salt and Water Conservation District. The graded interpretive trail is bordered with pieces of old railroad crossties. If you are following the trail clockwise, you will reach a cleared area at 0.2 mile, pass the lakeshore, and pass the grave site of Richard Henderson (1735–85) at 0.5 mile.

At Nutbush Bridge Campground is the 0.3-mile *Sycamore Springs Trail*. To access the trail from the I-85/NC-39 junction at Henderson, drive 4.5 miles north on NC-39 to Harris Crossroads. Turn right on Harris Road (SR-1308) and after 1.8 miles turn left at the campground entrance. Park in a pine grove at the first fork. The linear path through mature hardwoods, young pine, and honeysuckle exits on the right-fork road

0.1 mile from its origin. The trail gets its name from a spring that feeds a drain into Kerr Lake. The area has hazelnut bushes, which the Saponi Indians called "nutbush."

At Bullocksville Recreation Area is the 0.5-mile *Old Still Trail* (see map on page 23), a loop trail whose entrance is opposite the baseball field at the ranger station. At 0.3 mile, it turns sharply left to the ruins of an old illegal liquor still. Access is 3.3 miles west from Drewry on Bullocksville Road (SR-1366); access to Drewry is 2.3 miles west on Manson Road (SR-1237) from I-85, exit 223, or 2.4 miles west on Ridgeway Road (SR-1224) from I-85, exit 226. Both I-85 exits are north of Henderson.

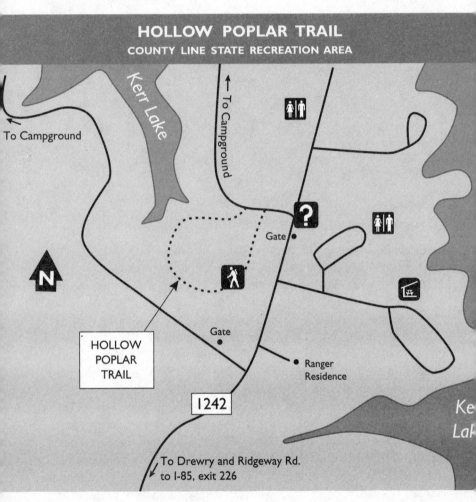

## HOLLOW POPLAR TRAIL
### COUNTY LINE STATE RECREATION AREA

Kerr Lake

To Campground

To Campground

Gate

HOLLOW POPLAR TRAIL

Gate

Ranger Residence

1242

To Drewry and Ridgeway Rd. to I-85, exit 226

Kerr Lake

N

*John H. Kerr Dam and Reservoir*
*Photo courtesy of North Carolina Travel and Tourism*

To reach County Line Recreation Area, use either of the accesses to Drewry and drive north on Drewry Road (SR-1200) for 3 miles. Turn left on Buchanan Road (SR-1202) and go 2.1 miles to the entrance. Park left of the fork at the ranger station to hike *Hollow Poplar Trail*. This 0.4-mile loop trail goes through a mature forest of oak, loblolly pine, sweet gum, and red maple. A large, partially hollow tulip poplar gives the trail its name.

*Raven Rock Loop Trail under cliffs beside Cape Fear River
in Raven Rock State Park*
Photo by Bob Bridges, The News and Observer

# Chapter 2

## TRAILS IN NORTH CAROLINA STATE PARKS, FORESTS, HISTORIC SITES, AND PRESERVES

The Department of Environment, Health, and Natural Resources (DEHNR) has seven Natural Resources divisions: Aquariums, Forest Resources, Marine Fisheries, Museum of Natural Sciences, Parks and Recreation, Soil and Water Conservation, and Zoological Park. The current administrative form was created in 1989, but a number of reorganizations preceded the change. For example, in 1955, the North Carolina legislature transferred all the state historic sites from Parks and Recreation to a new Department of Archives and History. In 1977, the legislature combined a number of agencies under the Department of Natural Resources and Community Development (DNRCD), which included the Division of Parks and Recreation.

The state parks system is divided into six units of management: state parks, lakes, recreation areas, rivers, trails, and natural areas. All the trails in the parks and natural areas in the Triangle area are covered in this chapter; the state recreation areas (SRAs) are covered in chapter 1.

Interest in the state's natural resources began in the late 19th century. An example is the establishment of a state Geological Survey in 1891 to determine North Carolina's mineral and forest resources. In 1905, the legislature reorganized the survey to create the North Carolina Geological and Economic Survey. When the legislature and Governor Locke Craig learned in 1914 that timber harvesting and forest fires were destroying such valuable areas as Mount Mitchell, the governor, a strong conservationist, went to the area for a personal inspection. The result was a bill passed in 1915 to create the state's first park, with a cost not to exceed $20,000. The management of Mount Mitchell State Park became the responsibility of the Geological and Economic Survey.

In 1925, the legislature expanded responsibility to fire prevention, reforestation, and maintenance of the state parks and forests when the Geological and Economic Survey was phased into the new Department of Conservation and Development. Acquisition was slow; only three of the Bladen Lakes areas were added to the list in the 1920s. But in the 1930s, federal assistance programs became available, particularly the Civilian Conservation Corps (CCC). Between 1935 and 1943, the state acquired six new parks. The congressional Recreation Area Study Act of 1936 became the blueprint for state parks systems, but the North Carolina legislature appropriated only sporadic funds. From 1945 to 1961, only Mount Jefferson was acquired.

Five state parks and a natural area were added in the 1960s. There was a notable increase in the 1970s, with 11 new parks, eight new natural areas, and the first SRA at Kerr Lake. This decade of growth came under the administrations of Governors Bob Scott and James E. Holshouser. Within a three-year period, the parklands nearly doubled thanks to the addition of 50,000 acres. Other advances during this period were the beginning of the state zoo, a trust fund for the natural areas, and the State Trails System Act of 1973, which created a master plan for implementing a statewide network of multiuse trails for hikers, bicyclists, equestrians, canoeists, and ORV users, as well as a seven-member citizens' Trail Committee to advise the director of Parks and Recreation.

During the 1980s, three SRAs (Jordan Lake, Falls Lake, and Fort Fisher) and one state park (Waynesborough) were opened. Legislative appropriations were increased but continued to be inadequate for maintenance and land acquisition. The *Winston-Salem Journal* editorialized in May 1987 that "North Carolina has a large financial investment and a priceless natural heritage in its parks. . . . It needs a master plan to overcome a starvation diet." The same month, the legislature passed the State Parks Act, led by State Senator Henson P. Barnes. The act established a master plan that "firmly defines the purpose of state parks and requires sound strategy in managing the system."

For many years, North Carolina has been at the bottom of national rankings for funding of park construction, staffing, and maintenance. Voters responded to this neglect on November 2, 1994, when they passed a $35 million bond referendum for a Parks and Recreation Trust Fund and Natural Heritage Trust Fund. It was a first in the agency's history and the largest single appropriation since its creation in 1915. Sixty-five percent of the recreation fund goes to state parks, 30 percent to matching funds for local park projects, and 5 percent to beach access. Phil McKnelly, the division's director, stated that trail supporters were among the many groups who made citizens aware of park system needs.

Among North Carolina's 29 parks, 23 have trails; the parks' 115 trails offer a total of 212.3 miles of hiking. With the exception of western parks that may close temporarily if there are unusually heavy snowstorms, all the parks are open all year. Most parks open daily at 8 A.M. They generally close at 6 P.M. November through February; at 7 P.M. in March and October; at 8 P.M. in April, May, and September; and at 9 P.M. June through August.

Rules are posted conspicuously in the parks. Alcohol, illegal drugs, and firearms are prohibited. Fishing is allowed, but a state license is necessary. Camping facilities (including those for primitive and youth-group camping) for individual parks in the Triangle are described in this chapter. When visiting a park, first go to the park office and request a brochure and maps to make your stay a pleasurable and educational experience.

In addition to the state parks, the Division of Parks and Recreation in the DEHNR administers 12 natural areas, four of which have visitor centers and designated trails. One of these, Hemlock Bluffs, is in the Triangle. In 1963, an increase in public pressure influenced the state to adopt principles for the natural-area system: to preserve, protect, extend, and develop natural areas of scientific, aesthetic, and geological value.

For information on state parks and state natural areas, contact the Division of Parks and Recreation, P.O. Box 27687 (512 North Salisbury Street), Raleigh, NC 27611 (919-733-7275 or 919-733-4181). For information on trails, contact the state Trails Coordinator, Division of Parks and Recreation, 12700 Bayleaf Church Road, Raleigh, NC 27614 (919-846-9991).

The Division of Forest Resources (another division of the DEHNR) administers five educational state forests. One of them, Clemmons Educational State Forest, is in the Triangle. The locations of the forests are diverse, but their purpose and facilities are generally the same. For example, they all have interpretive displays and trails, primitive walk-in campsites, and picnic areas. They serve as outdoor-living and environmental centers that teachers and other group leaders use as classrooms. Arrangements can be made with each ranger station for ranger-conducted programs. Campsites are free but require permits. Open season for most of the forests is March 15 to November 30; all are closed Mondays and Tuesdays.

There are 23 state historic sites administered by the Historic Sites Section, Division of Archives and History, Department of Cultural Resources. The sites offer visitor centers with artifacts, exhibits, and multimedia programs about such historic places as the Duke Homestead, Historic Halifax, and the Thomas Wolfe Memorial. The majority of the sites do not have admission charges. Those that have trails and are located in the Triangle area are described in this chapter. For more information, contact the Department of Cultural Resources, Raleigh, NC 27601 (919-733-7862).

Eight of the parks, forests, and historic sites in the Triangle area are covered here. Although the majority of trails in this chapter are short, they are important walks for educational and cultural purposes.

## BENTONVILLE BATTLEGROUND STATE HISTORIC SITE

Johnston County

After the capture of Savannah, Georgia, on December 20, 1864, General William T. Sherman's troops turned north to join General U. S. Grant's troops in Virginia. On the way, Sherman continued a swath of destruction, particularly in Columbia, South Carolina. The Battle of Bentonville is significant because it was the last major Confederate offensive and the largest battle fought in North Carolina. General Joseph E. Johnston, with less than half the number of Union troops, fought bravely but lost the battle, which took place from March 19 to March 21, 1865. The Confederates withdrew toward Smithfield with plans to protect Raleigh, the state capital, but the Union forces did not pursue them.

*Address and Access:* Bentonville Battleground State Historic Site, Box 27, Newton Grove, NC 28366 (910-594-0789). The entrance is 1.4 miles off US-701 on Cox Mill Road (SR-1008) 3 miles north of Newton Grove.

**Bentonville Battleground History Trail** *(0.2 mile)*
**Bentonville Battleground Trail** *(13.4 miles)*

*Length and Difficulty:* 13.6 miles combined, easy

*Special Features:* 27 history stations

*Trailheads and Description: Bentonville Battleground History Trail* is a self-guided walk that begins at the parking lot of the historic Harper House, near the field fortifications exhibit. It leads to the original trenches dug by Union forces on the first day of the battle.

From Harper House, begin the longer route by crossing Cox Mill Road (SR-1008) between trail markers #3 and #4; follow the public road. At 0.6 mile, turn left on SR-1192. You will reach a junction with SR-1008; turn right. At 2.7 miles, you will see the United Daughters of the Confederacy (UDC) monument to the Confederate soldiers. Turn left on SR-1194, which later merges with Devils Race Track Road (SR-1009); you will arrive at the Bentonville Community Building at 5.6 miles. Continue to marker #23 at 5.8 miles; here, Confederate cavalry was halted by the flooded Mill Creek. Return to the Bentonville Community Building and take the road to the left; after 0.1 mile, turn right at marker #24. At 7.1 miles, turn left at marker #25. Pass markers #26 and #27 and turn right on a private dirt road near a feed bin at 7.9 miles. Continue by the field's edge for 0.7 mile to a paved road and turn left at marker #28. You will reach SR-1008 at 9 miles; turn right and go 0.6 mile to Ebenezer Church to junction with SR-1009; a country store is across the road. Turn right and go 0.5 mile to marker #20. You will return to SR-1008 at 10.6 miles; follow it to the UDC marker at the SR-1194 junction at 11.6 miles. Return on SR-1008 to the starting point for a total of 13.4 miles.

---

# CLEMMONS EDUCATIONAL STATE FOREST
## Johnston County

A forest of 307 acres between Clayton and Garner, Clemmons Educational State Forest has study sites for rocks, trees, wildlife, watersheds, and forest management. Opened in 1976, it represents a transitional zone between the Piedmont and the coastal plain. A forestry center and exhibits explain the varied facilities of the area. Picnicking and group primitive camping facilities are available, and sections of the trails can be used by the handicapped. Visiting groups may choose from 15 ranger-conducted programs.

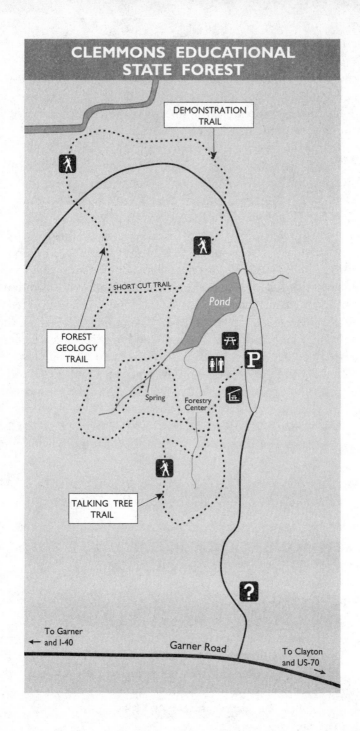

CLEMMONS EDUCATIONAL STATE FOREST

DEMONSTRATION TRAIL

SHORT CUT TRAIL

Pond

FOREST GEOLOGY TRAIL

Spring

Forestry Center

P

TALKING TREE TRAIL

?

To Garner and I-40

Garner Road

To Clayton and US-70

*One of the interpretive trails in Clemmons Educational State Forest*
Photo by Jim Bounds, *The* News and Observer

*Address and Access:* Forest Supervisor, Clemmons Educational State Forest, 2411 Garner Road, Clayton, NC 27520 (919-553-5651). Access is on Old US-70 (SR-1004) 1.5 miles north of the Clayton city limits and 4.2 miles north of US-70.

The 2.2-mile *Clemmons Demonstration Trail* begins at the parking lot. Follow the signs for 100 yards to a forest information board and another 100 yards to the forestry center and trail signboard. Turn right and follow the red blazes. At 0.2 mile, you will cross a stream near a short watershed path. At 0.3 mile, you will pass a shortcut trail; you will pass it again at 1.3 miles. The 0.8-mile, yellow-blazed *Clemmons Talking Tree Trail* loops from the trail signboard. An exceptionally well-designed trail, it provides push-button devices for recorded botanical information. Both trails have easy treadways. (USGS map: Clayton)

*View of Eno River from Holden's Mill Trail in Eno River State Park*

# ENO RIVER STATE PARK

## Durham and Orange Counties

Eno River State Park is a popular hiking and fishing area along 12 miles of the river between Hillsborough and Durham. Covering 2,304 acres, the park is segmented into four sections—Few's Ford, Cabe Lands Access, Cole Mill Road Access, and Pump Station Access—but the sections are similar, with floodplains, rocky bluffs, and some white water. Remnants of mill dams and rock piles illustrate the settlements of pioneer millers and farmers. Sycamore, river birch, and sweet gum are prominent on the riverside. Wildflowers are profuse; this is a park with a million trout lilies. Among the wildlife are deer, beaver, squirrel, fox, chipmunk, and turkey. Anglers will find Roanoke bass, largemouth bass, bream, redhorse sucker, and catfish. Activities at the park include picnicking and canoeing. Canoe-launching points are located below Pleasant Green Dam, Cole Mill Road, Few's Ford, and Guess Road. Group camping is allowed by reservation. All supplies including water and firewood must be packed in for 0.2 mile. Five backpack sites are available on a first-come basis for small groups or individuals. Accessing these sites requires a 1-mile hike. (USGS maps: Durham NW, Hillsborough)

*Address and Access:* Superintendent, Eno River State Park, 6101 Cole Mill Road, Durham, NC 27705 (919-383-1686). One access to the park office is 5.3 miles from I-85 in west Durham; drive north on Cole Mill Road (SR-1401 in Durham County, SR-1569 in Orange County). Look for the state park signs on I-85 between exits 172 and 173 because there was new highway construction in 1997.

## FEW'S FORD SECTION (South)
**Eno Nature Trail** *(0.3 mile)*
**Cox's Mountain Trail** *(3.7 miles)*
**Fanny's Ford Trail** *(1 mile)*

*Length and Difficulty:* 5 miles combined round-trip, moderate

*Trailheads and Description:* All these trails connect and are red-blazed. From the park office, drive to the second parking area, on the right.

Follow a well-maintained trail 0.1 mile to a junction on the left with *Eno Nature Trail*. (This self-guided trail is also called *Eno Trace*; it loops 0.3 mile through large hardwoods and has 12 interpretive posts.) Continue on *Cox's Mountain Trail* to cross the swinging footbridge over the Eno River. You will reach the Wilderness Shelter campsite, located on the left at 0.3 mile. At 0.7 mile, the trail forks; one fork leads left for a loop up the mountain and the other leads ahead on the old road. If hiking left, you will ascend and pass under a power line at 0.9 mile to Cox's Mountain. You will then descend to a stream at 1.2 miles and follow it downstream to the Eno River at 1.6 miles. Turn right and go downriver among river birch and beech. Turn right on an old wagon road at 2 miles, pass under a power line, and follow the old road in a forest with beds of running cedar. At 2.8 miles, you will junction with *Fanny's Ford Trail*, to the left. (*Fanny's Ford Trail* is a 1-mile loop by the riverbank and the pack-in primitive campsite. The trail's name comes from Fanny Breeze, a beloved black midwife and hospitable neighbor to the river community during and after the Civil War.) To complete the *Cox's Mountain Trail* loop, continue on the old road to the fork at 3 miles. Backtrack to the parking lot at 3.7 miles.

## FEW'S FORD SECTION (North)
**Buckquarter Creek Trail** (*1.5 miles*)
**Holden's Mill Trail** (*2.6 miles*)

*Length and Difficulty:* 4.1 miles combined round-trip, easy to moderate

*Trailheads and Description:* From the park office, drive to the first parking lot, on the right. Walk down to the Eno River, turn right, and head upriver to a loop fork at 0.1 mile. If hiking right, you will follow an old road; at 0.2 mile, turn left off the road into a forest of laurel, oak, and pine. You will join an old logging road at 0.5 mile, then pass through a cedar grove and curve left downstream of Buckquarter Creek. At 0.8 mile, you will reach a junction to the right with *Holden's Mill Trail*. (*Holden's Mill Trail* crosses Buckquarter Creek on a footbridge and after 160 yards ascends on an old farm road in a hardwood forest. You will pass rock piles from early farm clearings, then walk under a power line and descend to the Eno River at 1 mile; on the descent is a 0.6-mile loop upriver. To the right is the site of Holden's Mill. You will then return downriver on a scenic path of rocks and wildflowers near occasional

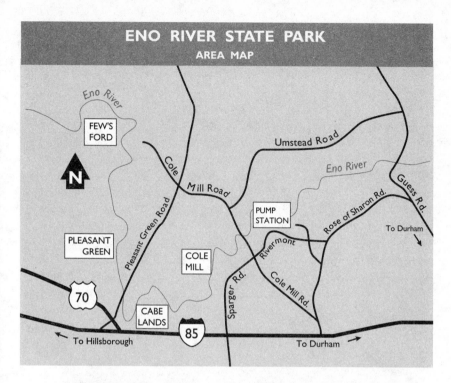

# ENO RIVER STATE PARK
## AREA MAP

Eno River

FEW'S FORD

**N**

Umstead Road

Cole

Mill Road

Eno River

Guess Rd.

PUMP STATION

Rose of Sharon Rd.

To Durham

Pleasant Green Road

PLEASANT GREEN

Rivermont

COLE MILL

Sparger Rd.

Cole Mill Rd.

**70**

CABE LANDS

**85**

← To Hillsborough

To Durham →

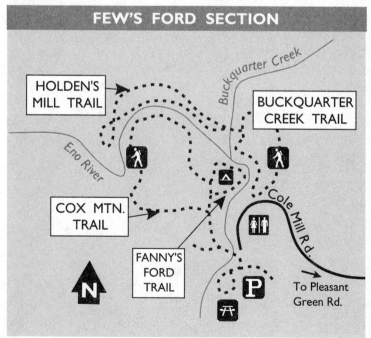

# FEW'S FORD SECTION

Buckquarter Creek

HOLDEN'S MILL TRAIL →

BUCKQUARTER CREEK TRAIL

Eno River

COX MTN. TRAIL

Cole Mill Rd.

FANNY'S FORD TRAIL

**N**

P

To Pleasant Green Rd.

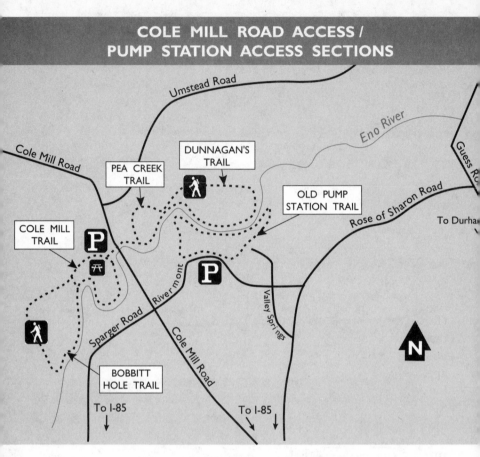

rapids and rejoin *Buckquarter Creek Trail* at 2.6 miles.) Continue downriver and complete *Buckquarter Creek Trail* after another 0.7 mile.

## COLE MILL ROAD ACCESS SECTION
**Pea Creek Trail** (*1.3 miles*)
**Dunnagan's Trail** (*1.8 miles*)
**Cole Mill Trail** (*1.2 miles*)
**Bobbitt Hole Trail** (*1.6 miles*)

*Length and Difficulty:* 7 miles combined round-trip, easy

*Trailheads and Description:* These trails are at Cole Mill Road Access, section 2. The activities offered at Cole Mill Road Access are picnicking, fishing, canoeing, and hiking. Access is as described above to the park office, except from I-85 go 3.2 miles and turn left on Umstead Road (SR-1449).

The trails connect, may overlap in parts, and are red-blazed. From the lower end of the parking area, follow the sign down to the Eno River; at 0.3 mile, you will reach *Pea Creek Trail* (left) and *Cole Mill Trail* (right). On *Pea Creek Trail*, you will pass under the Cole Mill Road bridge, then under a power line at 0.6 mile. You will reach Pea Creek in an area of wildflowers and ferns. At a footbridge is a junction with *Dunnagan's Trail*. After you cross Pea Creek, turn right along the Eno River. Turn left at the river and follow the bank downstream. Turn left just after the stone wall of the old pump station is visible across the river. Go uphill, circle back to Pea Creek on a ridge above the river, and pass through two old homesites. Complete *Pea Creek Trail* on a return to *Cole Mill Trail*.

Hike upriver on *Cole Mill Trail*. At 0.6 mile, you will junction with *Bobbitt Hole Trail*, which continues upriver; *Cole Mill Trail* turns right under a power line and rejoins *Bobbitt Hole Trail*, left, after 300 yards. (To the right, it is 0.4 mile on *Cole Mill Trail* to the upper parking lot and the picnic area.) If taking the higher elevation of *Bobbitt Hole Trail*, you will follow a beautiful, wide trail through pine, oak, and holly on the approach to the river. A right turn leads a few yards to a sharp curve in the river and the large, scenic pool called Bobbitt Hole after 0.9 mile. Return downriver. After 0.6 mile, you will junction with *Cole Mill Trail* for a return to the parking area.

## PUMP STATION ACCESS SECTION
### Old Pump Station Trail

*Length and Difficulty:* 1.5 miles, easy

*Trailhead and Description:* This loop trail is in the Pump Station Access, section 4. Access is as described above except as follows: after I-85, go 2.3 miles and turn right on Rivermont Road (SR-1402). Drive 0.6 mile to Nancy Rhodes Creek and park on the left.

Follow the trail sign to the remains of the old Durham Pump Station at 0.4 mile. Turn left upriver of the Eno, then make a sharp left at 1 mile. You will return under a power line and reach Rivermont Road at 1.3 miles. Turn left and follow the road back to the parking area.

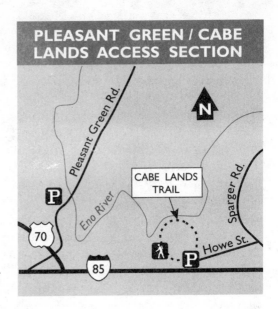

## CABE LANDS ACCESS SECTION
### Cabe Lands Trail

*Length and Difficulty:* 1.2 miles, easy

*Trailhead and Description:* This loop trail is at Cabe Lands Access, section 3. Access is as described above except as follows: after I-85, go 2.3 miles and turn left on Sprager Road (SR-1400). Go 1.3 miles, then turn right on Howe Street (Howell Road on county maps). After 0.5 mile, you will reach a parking space on the right.

Follow an old service road to the Eno River, passing carpets of periwinkle, ivy, and running cedar. You will reach the river at 0.4 mile; turn left. You will pass beaver cuts and old mill foundations at 0.4 mile, then cross a small stream and ascend to the point of origin.

## HEMLOCK BLUFFS NATURE PRESERVE
### Wake County

This 150-acre preserve received its name from eastern hemlock (*Tsuga canadensis*), a conifer usually not found farther east than Hanging Rock State Park, 100 miles northwest of Cary. In both locations, damp, cool, north-facing bluffs favor its survival from the Ice Age period of 10,000

*East Bluff Trail overlooks in Hemlock Bluff Nature Preserve*

to 18,000 years ago. In varying sizes, there are more than 200 of these beautiful evergreens, easily viewed from a trail network with observation decks near Swift Creek. (The 0.8-mile *Swift Creek Trail* on the north side of the stream is part of the Cary greenway system, not part of the Hemlock Bluffs trail network.) The hemlock trees, some as old as 400 years, are surrounded by other Appalachian Mountains plant species, among them yellow orchid, trillium, and chestnut oak, sometimes found in the western Piedmont.

This valuable and unique preserve was purchased by the state in 1976. Adjoining property is owned by the town of Cary, whose Parks and Recreation Department has developed and manages the entire preserve. Some assistance has been received from the Wake County Grant-in-Aid Program. At the entrance to the trail system is the Stevens Nature Center, completed in 1992 and named in honor of Colonel W. W. Stevens and his wife, Emily. The center has a park office, exhibit and classroom space, and a wildflower garden. Hours at the preserve are 9 A.M. to sunset daily; hours at the Stevens Nature Center vary according to the season. The exceptionally well-designed and well-maintained trail system is described below. (USGS map: Apex)

*Address and Access:* Hemlock Bluffs Nature Preserve, Box 8005 (2616 Kildaire Farm Road), Cary, NC 27512 (919-387-5980). To access the preserve from the junction of US-1 and US-64, go northeast on Tryon Road for 0.6 mile and turn right on Kildaire Farm Road. After 1.4 mile, turn right at the preserve entrance.

**East Bluff Trail** *(0.3 mile)*
**West Bluff Trail** *(0.7 mile)*
**Swift Creek Trail** *(0.8 mile)*
**Beech Tree Cove Trail** *(0.4 mile)*
**Chestnut Oak Trail** *(1.2 miles)*

*Length and Difficulty:* 2.1 miles combined round-trip, easy to moderate

*Trailheads and Description:* The trails' entrance is behind the Stevens Nature Center, where signboards provide trail information on distance (including overlap), direction, and blaze colors; if you are hiking from one trail to another in the two main loops, the combined distance is reduced. There are two trail brochures keyed to post numbers for the east and west trails. If you are following *East Bluff Trail*, markers #1 through #4 are about the bluffs and markers #5 through #14 describe the floodplain/Swift Creek area, wildlife, and wildflowers. The trail guide for the west trail covers the history of the upland forest, biological diversity, forest succession, and ecosystems. Quartz rocks are part of the ground cover along the trails, and chestnut oak is predominant among the trees.

If you make a right turn in the west trails, *West Bluff Trail* comes first.

## MEDOC MOUNTAIN STATE PARK
### Halifax County

This 2,286-acre park is on the granite fall line of the Piedmont, where the coastal-plain zone begins. The area was named for a grape-producing region in France; a large vineyard operated here in the 19th century. Although locally called a mountain because of its higher-than-usual elevation in the area, it is more a low ridge. Its summit is only 325 feet above sea level. Winding through the park is Little Fishing Creek, known for its stock of bluegill, largemouth and Roanoke bass, redbreast sunfish, and chain pickerel. Plant life is diverse here; it is unusual for laurel to be this far east.

Among the activities in the park are fishing, picnicking, hiking, and tent camping. The camping facilities include tables, grills, tent pads, a central water source, and hot showers. Camping facilities for groups and families are available mid-March through November; reservations are required for groups. (USGS maps: Hollister, Aurelian Springs, Essex)

*Address and Access:* Superintendent, Medoc Mountain State Park, P.O. Box 400, Hollister, NC 27844 (919-445-2280). The park office is on Medoc Mountain Road (SR-1002) 4.6 miles east of the NC-561 intersection at Hollister and 2 miles west of NC-48.

*Support Facilities:* Groceries and gasoline are available in Hollister.

**Summit Trail** (*2.9 miles*)
**Dam Site Loop Trail** (*0.9 mile*)

*Length and Difficulty:* 3.8 miles combined round-trip, easy

*Beech trees in Medoc Mountain State Park*
*Photo by Jim Page*

*Trailheads and Description:* From the park office parking lot, follow the trail sign. After 125 yards, turn left to begin the loop of *Summit Trail*. At 0.5 mile, you will cross Rocky Spring Branch. You will then reach the east bank of Little Fishing Creek at 0.7 mile. Turn right and go upstream. You will pass a large granite outcropping—the core of the summit—at

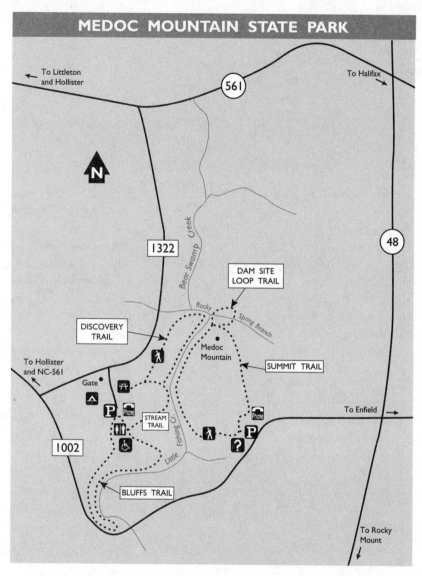

To Littleton
and Hollister ←

To Halifax →

561

N

1322

Bear Swamp Creek

DAM SITE
LOOP TRAIL

48

Rocky

Spring Branch

DISCOVERY
TRAIL

Medoc
Mountain

SUMMIT TRAIL

To Hollister
and NC-561 ←

Gate

Phone

STREAM
TRAIL

P

Phone

To Enfield →

1002

Little Fishing Cr.

P

?

BLUFFS TRAIL

To Rocky
Mount ↓

1.4 miles. After a few yards, the trail ascends 0.1 mile to the right to reach the peak. But if you want to include *Dam Site Loop Trail*, continue ahead (north) and pass an artesian well. You will pass the ruins of a dam built by the Boy Scouts in the early 1920s and the ruins of another dam upstream. Circle back to *Summit Trail* through groves of laurel at 2.5 miles. You will follow a gravel road, then turn from it at 3.1 miles. You will then pass an old cemetery, on the left, and return to the parking lot.

**Stream Trail** *(2.2 miles)*
**Discovery Trail** *(0.1 mile)*
**Bluffs Trail** *(2.8 miles)*

*Length and Difficulty:* 5.1 miles combined, easy

*Trailheads and Description:* Access these connecting trails by driving 2.2 miles west from the park office on SR-1002 to Medoc State Park Road (SR-1322). Turn right and follow the park signs 1 mile to the picnic parking area.

From the parking area, walk 60 yards right of the picnic shelter to the trail sign. *Stream Trail* is to the left. (*Bluffs Trail* is to the right.) *Stream Trail* is beautiful, well designed, and carefully maintained. It passes through a forest of loblolly pine, oak, and beech with an understory of laurel, holly, and aromatic bayberry. Rattlesnake orchid, partridgeberry, and running cedar are part of the ground cover. At 0.2 mile, you will arrive at Little Fishing Creek and head upstream. At 0.4 mile, you will junction with *Discovery Trail*. Proceed 0.3 mile left to exit to the picnic and parking area.

To include *Discovery Trail*, turn right. At 1.2 miles, you will reach a confluence with Bear Swamp Creek. You will then enter an open area with kudzu and trumpet vine at 1.6 miles. Exit the forest at 2 miles and cross the picnic grounds to the parking area at 2.2 miles.

On *Bluffs Trail*, you will pass through an old field on a wide, manicured trail leading into a forest. At 0.4 mile, turn right (downstream) by Little Fishing Creek. You will pass through large loblolly pine, beech, river birch, and oak, then climb to a steep bluff at 1 mile. You will reach the highest bluff (over 60 feet) at 1.4 miles. You will then descend, bear right on a return ridge, cross a stream at 2.6 miles, and return to the parking lot at 2.8 miles.

## RAVEN ROCK STATE PARK
### Harnett County

Established in 1970, Raven Rock State Park is a 3,300-acre wilderness-type forest. The Cape Fear River runs through its center. A major geological feature of the area is the 152-foot-high crystalline rock jutting out toward the river. Ravens once nested here, thus the park's name. It is unusual for rhododendron and laurel to grow this far east. The park also features a diverse and long list of Piedmont and coastal-plain plants. Some of the wild animals and birds present are osprey, eagle, owl, squirrel, raccoon, salamander, and deer. Prominent fish are largemouth bass, catfish, and sunfish. Activities in the park include picnicking, hiking, fishing, and primitive backpack camping. All gear and supplies (including water) must be carried to the camps; registration is required at the park office. There are bridle trails on the north side of the river; directions and regulations are available from the park office. (USGS map: Mamers)

*Address and Access:* Superintendent, Raven Rock State Park, Route 3, Box 1005, Lillington, NC 27546 (910-893-4888). Access the park by driving 3 miles off US-421 on Raven Rock Park Road (SR-1314) 6 miles west of Lillington.

**Raven Rock Loop Trail** (2.1 miles)
**American Beech Nature Trail** (0.5 mile)
**Little Creek Loop Trail** (1.4 miles)
**Fish Traps Trail** (1.2 miles, round-trip)
**Northington's Ferry Trail** (2.2 miles, round-trip)

*Length and Difficulty:* 7.4 miles combined round-trip, easy to moderate

*Special Feature:* Raven Rock overhang

*Trailhead and Description:* From the parking lot, follow the Raven Rock sign on the east side of the lot. A junction with *American Beech Nature Trail* is to the right. (*American Beech Nature Trail* descends and crosses a small stream through poplar, sweet gum, red maple, beech, sweet bay, laurel, and oak. It returns on the east side of the picnic area.) At 0.8 mile, *Raven Rock Loop Trail* junctions with *Little Creek Loop Trail*, to the right. (*Little Creek Loop Trail* descends downstream by Little Creek for 0.7 mile to a canoe camp.) Downriver, it is another 0.5 mile on *Raven Rock Loop Trail* to a group backpack campsite. You will reach scenic Raven Rock at 0.9 mile. Descend on stairways to the riverbank and rock overhangs; return on the steps, but take a right turn at the top. You will arrive at a scenic overlook of the Cape Fear River at 1.1 mile, then junction

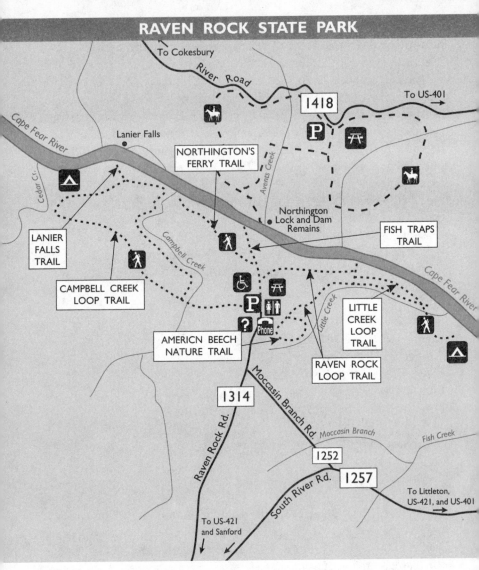

To Cokesbury

River Road

To US-401

1418

Cape Fear River

Lanier Falls

NORTHINGTON'S
FERRY TRAIL

Cedar Cr.

Avents Creek

Northington
Lock and Dam
Remains

FISH TRAPS
TRAIL

Cape Fear River

LANIER
FALLS
TRAIL

Campbell Creek

CAMPBELL CREEK
LOOP TRAIL

Little Creek

LITTLE
CREEK
LOOP
TRAIL

P

Phone

AMERICN BEECH
NATURE TRAIL

RAVEN ROCK
LOOP TRAIL

1314

Raven Rock Rd.

Moccasin Branch Rd.

Moccasin Branch

Fish Creek

1252

South River Rd.

1257

To Littleton,
US-421, and US-401

To US-421
and Sanford

sharply right with *Fish Traps Trail* and *Northington's Ferry Trail* at 1.7 miles. (*Fish Traps Trail*—named for the trap baskets Indians placed at the rapids to catch fish—leads to a rock outcrop beside the river at 1.1 miles; backtrack. *Northington's Ferry Trail* follows a wide, easy route to the mouth of Campbell Creek—also called Camels Creek—the site of a Cape Fear River ferry crossing linking Raleigh and Fayetteville as early as 1770; backtrack.) Continue on *Raven Rock Loop Trail* on an old woods road to the parking area.

**Campbell Creek Loop Trail** (*5.1 miles*)
**Lanier Falls Trail** (*0.4 mile*)

*Length and Difficulty:* 5.5 miles combined round-trip, easy to moderate

*Trailheads and Description:* From the parking lot, follow the old service road 45 yards north and turn left into young growth that enters an older forest. You will descend gradually in an oak/hickory forest to a footbridge over Campbell Creek at 0.7 mile. Here, the trail loops right or left. If taking the left route, you will ascend and descend on low ridges through sections of laurel to junction with the former *Buckhorn Trail* at 2.1 miles. (*Buckhorn Trail* is covered in chapter 5; the section adjoining Raven Rock State Park has been abandoned.) A park service road comes in from the left and joins *Campbell Creek Loop Trail*, right. Descend to the primitive campsites on the left at 2.3 miles and *Lanier Falls Trail*, located on the left at 2.5 miles. (The 0.2-mile *Lanier Falls Trail* leads to a scenic rock outcrop at the Cape Fear River; backtrack.) Follow *Campbell Creek Loop Trail* to the mouth of Campbell Creek and continue upstream to rejoin the access route at the bridge at 4.4 miles.

## WAYNESBOROUGH STATE PARK
Wayne County

One of the state's newest parks, Waynesborough State Park began in 1986 at the site of historic Waynesborough, founded in 1787. The park has a visitor center with history exhibits, a picnic area, the 0.6-mile *Loop Trail* on a floodplain, a boat dock at the Neuse River, a village of 19th-century houses, a law office dating from 1868, and a one-room school dating from 1911. A total of 8.7 miles of the signed *Mountains-to-Sea Trail* circles part of the park, crosses US-117 into the city of Goldsboro, joins *Stoney Creek Trail*, and passes downstream to Slocum Road at an entrance to Seymour Johnson Air Force Base; see chapter 4 for coverage of Goldsboro. (USGS maps: Goldsboro SE, Goldsboro SW)

*Address and Access:* Waynesborough State Park, 801 US-117 South, Goldsboro, NC 27530 (919-580-9391 or 919-778-6234). From the junction of US-70 and US-117, drive south on US-117 for 2 miles to the entrance, on the right.

# WILLIAM B. UMSTEAD STATE PARK
## Wake County

William B. Umstead State Park covers 5,381 acres: 4,026 in the Crabtree Creek (northern) section and 1,355 in the Reedy Creek (southern) section. Crabtree Creek runs west to east through the park and separates the two sections. Among the largest of North Carolina's state parks, Umstead is a valuable oasis in the center of a fast-developing metropolitan area. Adjoining on the west is Raleigh/Durham International Airport, on the north is US-70, and on the south is I-40.

A former CCC camp, the park's original 5,088 acres were deeded to the state by the federal government for a dollar in 1943. The property was designated Crabtree Creek State Park but in 1955 was renamed in honor of the former governor.

In the Reedy Creek section is Piedmont Beech Natural Area, a 50-acre tract containing American beech (*Fagus grandifolia*), some of which are more than 300 years old. The tract is included in the National Registry of Natural Landmarks. Access is by permit only.

Sycamore Creek runs through the park from northwest to southeast and empties into Crabtree Creek. Tributaries such as Pott's Branch, Reedy Creek, and Turkey Creek flow into the main creeks. The park is hilly and rocky. Quartz rock piles indicate the presence of farmers in the last century and the early part of the 1900s. There are three lakes in the park: Big Lake, Sycamore Lake, and Reedy Creek Lake. Fishing for bass, bluegill, and crappie is allowed, but swimming is permitted only at the park's group campsites. Large stands of mature oak, poplar, and loblolly pine provide a canopy for dogwood, redbud, laurel, and sourwood. Beaver, deer, squirrel, and raccoon are among the mammals in the park. Recreational activities include fishing, camping, hiking, picnicking, horseback riding, bicycling, and nature study. The park offers three organized group camps and a lodge.

Both park sections offer equestrian and hiking trails; there are 16 miles of trails on gated park gravel roads. Their access points are off Ebenezer Church Road from US-70 (from the north), from Old Reedy Creek Road off Ebenezer Church Road (from the southeast), and off Old Reedy Creek Road from Weston Parkway (from the southwest). *Big Lake Handicapped Trail*, a 0.2-mile (one-way) paved trail offering scenic beauty and fishing for disabled persons, is in the Crabtree Creek section. It crosses the dam

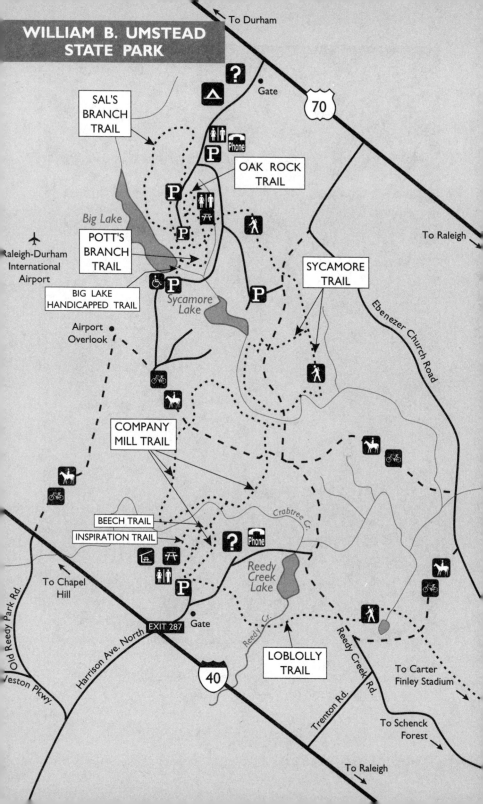

*Fishing in Big Lake near Sal's Branch Trail, Umstead State Park*
Photo by Bill Russ, North Carolina Travel and Tourism

and a bridge over the spillway to the bathhouse. Access the trail by driving the road past the park office to a parking lot on the right. *Loblolly Trail* is a 6-mile linear trail, 2.7 miles (one-way) of which are in William B. Umstead State Park; its other mileage is in the city of Raleigh. The park access is at the northeast corner of the parking lot at the Reedy Creek section; a signboard shows its direction beginning at a large white oak tree. Its southern access is at gate D of Carter-Finley Stadium; see the coverage of Raleigh in chapter 4. (USGS maps: Cary, Raleigh W, Durham SE)

*Address and Access:* William B. Umstead State Park, Route 8, Box 130, Raleigh, NC 27612 (919-787-3033). Access to the Crabtree Creek section entrance is on US-70; drive 6 miles west from the junction with I-40. To reach the Reedy Creek section entrance from the Crabtree Creek entrance on US-70, drive 1 mile west to Aviation Parkway; turn left, go 4 miles to I-40, turn left on I-40, go 3.6 miles to exit 287 at Harrison Avenue, and turn left (north). From the I-40 junction at Wade Avenue in Raleigh, drive 4 miles west to exit 287 and turn right.


**Sal's Branch Trail** *(2.4 miles)*
**Pott's Branch Trail** *(1 mile)*
**Oak Rock Trail** *(0.7 mile)*

*Length and Difficulty:* 4.1 miles combined round-trip, easy to moderate

*Trailheads and Description:* In the Crabtree Creek section, park at the lower parking and picnic area—the area nearest Big Lake. At the lower (southwest) corner of the lot, descend 110 yards on a wide trail with steps to a junction on the left with the orange-diamond-blazed *Pott's Branch Trail*. Another 75 feet down the steps, you will reach a junction on the right with the orange-circle-blazed *Sal's Branch Trail*. A descent of another 60 feet will bring you to the paved *Big Lake Handicapped Trail*, right and left, described in the introduction above.

Follow *Sal's Creek Trail* through loblolly pine and hardwoods with Christmas fern and running cedar on the forest floor. You will cross a service road at 0.5 mile and pass a beech grove by the branch at 0.8 mile. Turn uphill sharply at 1.9 miles to complete the loop at 2.4 miles.

Follow *Pott's Branch Trail* through tall loblolly pine for 0.3 mile, where the trail turns left away from Sycamore Creek and parallels Pott's Branch.

At 0.5 mile, you will intersect *Sycamore Trail*. (To the left, *Sycamore Trail* goes up the steps and 0.2 mile through the picnic area to the parking lot. To the right, it goes across Pott's Branch on its long loop; see the description below.) As you continue on *Pott's Branch Trail*, notice the stone dam remains from CCC work on the right. You will pass a large observation deck, located on the right, and ascend to the upper parking lot at 1 mile.

## Sycamore Trail

*Length and Difficulty:* 6.5 miles, easy to moderate

*Trailhead and Description:* Park at the lower parking lot and follow the trail signs up the steps to the picnic area. You will pass between two large picnic shelters and descend on wide steps to cross *Pott's Branch Trail* and Pott's Branch at 0.2 mile. Follow the blue-blazed trail upstream to cross Sycamore Lake Road at 0.5 mile. The path heads through a forest of oak, maple, pine, and running cedar and passes under a power line at 1.5 miles. Ahead is a former homesite in a grove of huge white oak and wisteria. Exit to a park road and horse trail; to the left is King Cemetery and a gate to Graylyn Road (a spur off Ebenezer Road). You will cross the road and descend among more large white oak, then cross a horse trail. At 1.9 miles, *Sycamore Trail* forks for a loop. If turning left, you will descend into a hollow featuring holly and beech, then cross at least four footbridges at the bank of a rocky bluff among wild orchid, crested dwarf iris, and ferns. You will then cross more footbridges, curve right, and ascend a ridge with quartz footing to parallel Sycamore Creek. At 3.4 miles, you will descend to cross a park road used by equestrians and bikers. (To the left, across the CCC bridge and immediately right, is a 280-foot spur trail that connects with *Company Mill Trail*.) After crossing a flat area, you will ascend a rocky hillside, pass the edge of a high bluff, then descend to the creek bank. You will pass under a power line at 4.1 miles, then ascend steeply on switchbacks. On the hilltop, you will cross a park road at 4.4 miles. At 4.6 miles, you will return to the loop for a backtrack to the parking lot at 6.5 miles.

**Company Mill Trail** *(5.3 miles)*
**Inspiration Trail** *(0.5 mile)*
**Beech Trail** *(0.4 mile)*

*Length and Difficulty:* 6.2 miles combined round-trip, easy to moderate

*Trailheads and Description:* From the Reedy Creek section parking lot, walk to the northwest corner and descend to a display board at the edge of the woods. At 0.1 mile is a large stone picnic shelter in the picnic area. To the right is the trailhead for *Company Mill Trail*. To the left is the blue-diamond-blazed *Inspiration Trail*. *Inspiration Trail* descends to a streamlet, turns left, parallels the ravine, curves up the hill, and junctions left with the blue-circle-blazed *Beech Trail*, which connects *Inspiration Trail* with *Company Mill Trail*. Turn right and return to the picnic shelter and the trailhead for *Company Mill Trail* at 0.5 mile.

The orange-blazed *Company Mill Trail* descends and ascends three ridges on the descent to the Crabtree Creek steel footbridge at 0.6 mile. On the way, you will observe quartz rock piles made by pioneer farmers on the rocky slopes and pass a junction on the left with *Beech Trail* at 0.3 mile. After crossing the footbridge, turn right or left for a loop. If hiking right, you will descend between rock ledges on the left and the creek on the right. At 0.7 mile are rapids and remnants of the dam. A millstone is left of the trail. Turn left at 1.2 miles and follow a tributary, crossing it a number of times among tall trees, many of them beech. Descend from the ridge to the south bank of Sycamore Creek and turn left at 2.1 miles. (To the right, it is 280 feet to a park road; going left over a bridge leads to a junction with *Sycamore Trail*, right and left.) Stay near the creek side, partly on a rim of a former millrace. Maidenhair fern, buckeye, and black cohosh adorn the trail. Rock remnants of George Lynn Mill Dam are to the right. You will leave the creek on switchbacks at 2.2 miles. You will come to a ridge, then descend on switchbacks to a small stream, then ascend to the top of the ridge at 2.7 miles. You will cross a park service road at 3.1 miles and gradually descend to the bank of Crabtree Creek at 4.2 miles. You will pass right of a rock slope and complete the loop at 4.7 miles. Cross the high footbridge over the creek and ascend to the picnic shelter at 5.3 miles.

*View from Lake Crabtree Trail, Lake Crabtree County Park*

# Chapter 3

## TRAILS IN COUNTY PARKS AND
## RECREATION AREAS

Fifty-nine of the state's 100 counties have parks and recreation departments. They operate as a separate public unit in each county, usually under a county board of commissioners. A few counties and cities combine their departments or resources to provide joint services or special projects. Examples are Clinton and Sampson County, Henderson and Vance County, and Sanford and Lee County. Because of population needs and available funding, county parks vary in size, facilities, and scope, from simple day-use picnic areas to complex recreational centers such as Tanglewood in Forsyth County.

When the President's Commission on Americans Outdoors reported its findings in 1986, it showed rapid expansion in a number of North Carolina cities. With an increase in population and less space in the cities for outdoor recreation, county parks are becoming more vital for green space. The report also showed a demographic trend toward a fast-growing older segment of the population and a desire for recreation close to home. Mecklenburg and Forsyth are examples of counties preparing for this trend. Mecklenburg's diverse parks and greenways system, the largest in the state, will become what Elisabeth Hair, former chair of the Board of County Commissioners, called "Charlotte's green necklace." In Forsyth County, greenways will connect the county's towns to a greenway network in the city of Winston-Salem. A number of county parks and recreation departments have constructed physical-fitness trails. Others, such as Craven County's department, do not own property but maintain exercise trails on public-school property.

To receive the *North Carolina Parks and Recreation Directory*, which contains listings for the state's counties and cities with parks, contact the Division of Parks and Recreation, Box 27687, Raleigh, NC 27687 (919-733-PARK) or call 919-515-7118 at North Carolina State University.

# ALAMANCE COUNTY

The Alamance County Recreation and Parks Department is well known for its scenic and splendid network of 150 miles of bicycle trail routes. Among its seven trails is *Route 74*, a 59-mile route that circles the county and connects with all the other bike routes. Plans may be to connect the loop with *Mountains-to-Sea Trail* in the northern part of the county. *Mountains-to-Sea Bike Route* #2 passes through the southern part of the county on its way from Murphy to Manteo. The county's bicycle trails were planned to connect historic sites and parks, one of which is described below. For information, contact the Recreation and Parks Department, 217 College Street, Graham, NC 27253 (910-570-6760, office; 910-570-6759, camp reservations).

## CEDAROCK PARK

This historic and highly diversified 414-acre park contains the Cedarock Park Center, used for conferences and workshops in the Paul Stevens homestead, and Cedarock Historical Farm, dating from the 1830s. Recreational facilities include two disk golf courses; basketball and volleyball courts; picnic areas, some with shelters; a fishing pond; walk-in campsites for primitive camping (permits are required); a ropes obstacle course; playgrounds; and a variety of trails. The 4.3-mile *Equestrian Trail* circles the perimeter of the park. On the northwest side of the circle is the 0.25-mile *Hiking Trail* near the Wellspring Disk Golf Course. Access to the horse trail is near Cedarock Historical Farm. A parking area near picnic shelter #3 gives access to the 1.3-mile *Mountain Bike Trail*. Color-coded interconnecting trail loops are described below. The park is open all year. (USGS map: Snow Camp)

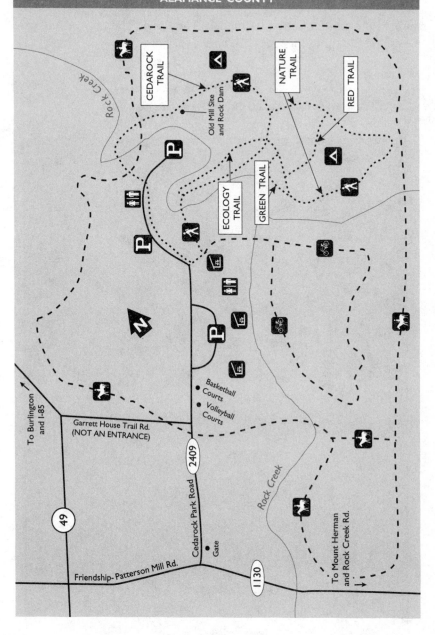

# CEDAROCK PARK
## ALAMANCE COUNTY

Rock Creek

CEDAROCK TRAIL

NATURE TRAIL

RED TRAIL

Old Mill Site and Rock Dam

ECOLOGY TRAIL

GREEN TRAIL

P

P

P

N

Basketball Courts

Volleyball Courts

To Burlington and I-85

Garrett House Trail Rd. (NOT AN ENTRANCE)

Cedarock Park Road

2409

Gate

49

Friendship-Patterson Mill Rd.

Rock Creek

1130

To Mount Herman and Rock Creek Rd.

*Access:* From the junction of I-85/40 and NC-49 in Burlington (exit 145A from the west, exit 145 from the east), go nearly 6 miles on NC-49 to the junction with Friendship-Patterson Mill Road; turn left. Drive 0.3 mile to the park entrance, on the left. The ranger station is at the first house on the right, the Garrett homestead.

*Crossing Rock Creek Bridge on Cedarock Trail*

**Cedarock Trail** *(2.2 miles)*
**Ecology Trail** *(0.5 mile)*
**Nature Trail** *(0.8 mile)*
**Green Trail** *(0.13 mile)*
**Red Trail** *(0.16 mile)*

*Length and Difficulty:* 3.9 miles combined, easy

*Trailheads and Description:* From the picnic area parking lot, begin at shelter #3 at the trail signboard. (To the right is the white-marked *Mountain Bike Trail*, which descends to a fork after 75 yards. Hiking in either direction takes you to a meadow and a footbridge over Rock Creek. A loop entirely in the forest follows.)

Begin the yellow-blazed *Cedarock Trail* to the left of the trail signboard. The trail descends to cross a narrow footbridge over Rock Creek at 0.1 mile in a meadow of wildflowers. After a few yards, you will enter a forest and junction with the brown-blazed *Ecology Trail*, to the left; this trail runs jointly with *Cedarock Trail* for a distance. At 0.4 mile, *Ecology Trail* turns left to complete its loop. Along the way, it skirts a bend of Rock Creek.

To the right is the blue-blazed *Nature Trail*. If following it, look for *Green Trail* to the right after a few yards; *Green Trail* makes a short curve among ferns, wild azalea, and rock formations beside a cascading stream. Turn left and return to *Nature Trail*. (In the short distance between the trailheads of *Green Trail*, *Nature Trail* junctions with the western trailhead of *Red Trail*, a connector.) Continue upstream on *Nature Trail*; you will pass through an oak/hickory forest and scattered pine. Ferns, hepatica, and wild orchid are prominent near the stream. At 0.4 mile, you will leave the scenic stream and ascend gently over a ridge. You will junction left with *Red Trail* to a walk-in campsite at 0.6 mile, then cross a small footbridge and rejoin *Cedarock Trail* at 0.7 mile.

If taking a left, you will rock-hop a small stream and junction with *Ecology Trail* for a return to the trail signboard. If continuing to the right on *Cedarock Trail*, you will soon leave the forest, cross through a meadow near a tent campground, reenter the forest, and reach an old mill dam on the left. You will then cross *Equestrian Trail* and a bridge at Elmo's Crossing. You will enter a meadow of wildflowers, including star-of-Bethlehem (*Ipheion uniflorum*), at 2 miles. After a bridge over a small stream, you will pass a maintenance area, reach the park road, and return to the parking lot near picnic shelter #3 at 2.2 miles.

# LEE COUNTY

## SAN-LEE PARK

This park is composed of 125 acres of forest, lakes, old waterworks, trails, picnic areas, and family (RV) and group campgrounds. It also offers an amphitheater, a boat launch, boat rentals, a volleyball court, and other facilities. All the trails are well designed and maintained. The park is open all year. (USGS map: Sanford)

*Address and Access:* Director, Parks and Recreation Department, Box 698, Sanford, NC 27330 (919-775-2107). The telephone number for San-Lee Park is 919-776-6221. At the junction of US-1 Business and Charlotte Avenue (US-421/NC-87/42), take Charlotte Avenue east for 1.2 miles to Grapeviney Road (also called San-Lee Drive, SR-1509); turn right. After 2.2 miles, turn right on Pumping Station Road (SR-1510) and go 0.6 mile to the park entrance, on the right.


**Muir Nature Trail** *(1.1 miles)*
**Gatewood Trail** *(0.8 mile)*
**Hidden Glen Loop Trail** *(0.2 mile)*
**Thoreau Trail** *(0.9 mile)*

*Length and Difficulty:* 3 miles combined, easy

*Trailheads and Description:* From the parking lot by Miner's Creek, cross the bridge, turn right, and follow the *Muir Nature Trail* signs into the woods; you have a choice of an upper or lower loop. At 0.5 mile, turn left at the lake's edge at the steps. You will pass through rocks, hardwoods, softwoods, and wildflowers on the return.

You can hike a few yards or park at the refreshment stand to hike the other trails. Follow the campground road to the Colter Amphitheater signs. Turn right on *Gatewood Trail*. At 0.3 mile, you will junction with *Thoreau Trail*, on the right. Turn left to reach a junction with *Hidden Glen Loop Trail* at 0.5 mile. You will pass the Aldo Leopold Wilderness group campground on the return. *Thoreau Trail* begins at the boat launch near the bridge over Moccasin Pond. Cross the bridge and follow the shoreline to the left. You will cross a bridge over Crawdad Creek and junction with *Gatewood Trail* at 0.6 mile. Return either left (the shorter route) or right.

# WAKE COUNTY

Wake County has two major parks with pedestrian trails. Like Mecklenburg County, Wake is largely urbanized. Like Charlotte, Raleigh is centrally located. The difference between the two counties is that in Wake the city and county parks are in separate departments. See chapter 4 for information on Raleigh trails. For information on Wake County trails, contact the Wake County Parks and Recreation Department, Box 550, Suite 1000, Wake County Office Building, Raleigh, NC 27602 (919-856-6670).

## BLUE JAY POINT COUNTY PARK

Blue Jay Point County Park is located on a peninsula at Falls Lake. It offers ball fields, a playground, picnic areas, a lodge, and the Center for Environmental Education. The latter was established for the purpose of outdoor education for schoolchildren and for hosting training programs. Part of *Falls Lake Trail* (see chapter 1) passes around the park's lake boundary. Short connector trails (*Blue Jay Point Trail*, *Sandy Point Trail*, and *Laurel Trail*, each 0.2 mile in length) and a paved trail for the physically disabled descend to meet the 3.1-mile segment of *Falls Lake Trail*.
   *Address and Access:* Blue Jay Point County Park, 3200 Pleasant Union Church Road, Raleigh, NC 27614 (919-870-4330). Access is off Six Forks Road 1.5 miles south of its junction with NC-98 and 1.5 miles north of its junction with Possum Track Road.

## LAKE CRABTREE COUNTY PARK

Bordering I-40 at the western edge of the county, this 215-acre park adjoins 500-acre Lake Crabtree. The park provides picnic areas with shelters, playgrounds, fishing piers, boat rentals, and boat ramps.
   The 0.6-mile *Old Beech Nature Trail* (with markers) is located in a damp

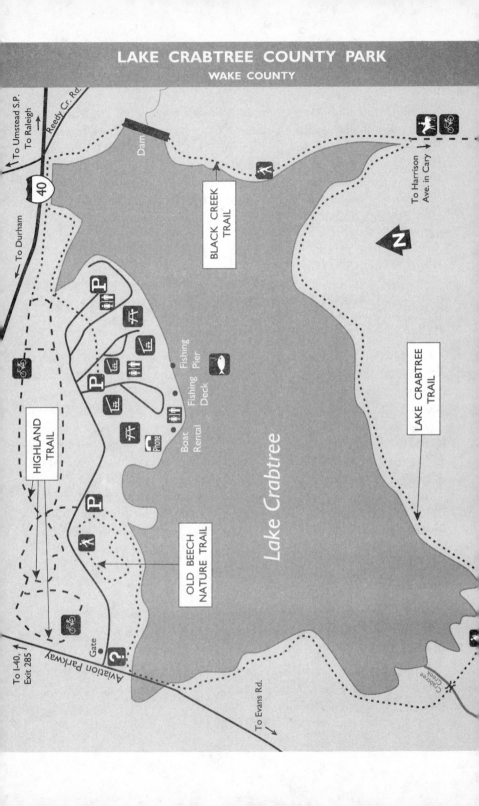

# LAKE CRABTREE COUNTY PARK

## WAKE COUNTY

To Umstead S.P.
To Raleigh

Reedy Cr. Rd.

40

To Durham

Dam

BLACK CREEK TRAIL

N

To Harrison Ave. in Cary

Fishing Pier

Fishing Deck

Boat Rental

Phone

LAKE CRABTREE TRAIL

HIGHLAND TRAIL

Lake Crabtree

OLD BEECH NATURE TRAIL

Gate

Aviation Parkway

To I-40, Exit 285

To Evans Rd.

Crabtree Creek

area. It has boardwalks among oak, pine, sweet gum, and maple (one of which has three "legs" and is located at 0.3 mile). Access is at the first parking lot to the right after you enter the park.

Across the road is a foot route with switchbacks up the hill to *Highland Trail*. This trail has three loops. Loop #1 (1.3 miles in length) is to the right. Loops #2 and #3 are also to the right; loop #2 is 0.5 mile in length and, farther west, loop #3 is 1 mile in length. Biking is allowed in the loops. Access is off the road to the boat ramp, or paralleling I-40 from Old Reedy Creek Road at *Lake Crabtree Trail* and *Black Creek Trail* (see below).

The sound of traffic from I-40 and Raleigh/Durham International Airport is prominent throughout the park. The park's longest hiking trail is *Lake Crabtree Trail*, described below. (USGS map: Cary)

*Address and Access:* Lake Crabtree County Park, 1400 Aviation Parkway, Morrisville, NC 27560 (919-460-3390). Access is from I-40, exit 285; drive south on Aviation Parkway 0.3 mile and turn left.

## Lake Crabtree Trail

*Length and Difficulty:* 5.4 miles, easy to moderate

*Trailhead and Description:* If parking at the trailhead for the nature trail (the closest access to the western trailhead of *Lake Crabtree Trail*) and entering the eastern trailhead, walk east on the main park road 0.3 mile to a road to the right that leads to the boat-rental and fishing dock. At the first parking lot, you will notice the trailhead and signboard to the left. At 0.2 mile, you will cross a footbridge and turn right on the blue-blazed trail. Among the forest of young pine and oak, you will pass through redbud, hazelnut, sumac, and witch hazel. At 0.4 mile is an observation deck. Stay near the lake's edge and avoid the routes to the left, which connect with *Highland Trail*. At 0.8 mile, you will parallel I-40, where cow-itch vine hugs the rocks on the lakeside. You will then pass through a gated fence at 1 mile and ascend to the top of Lake Crabtree Dam. Here is a signboard of information. To the left is a gate at Old Reedy Creek Road. (Access to Old Reedy Creek Road is off I-40, exit 287; drive south on Harrison Avenue for 0.4 mile, turn right on Weston Parkway, go 0.5 mile, turn right, and go 0.8 mile to the road-shoulder parking at the dam.)

Continue by following the asphalt-surfaced, 2.5-mile *Black Creek Trail*

*Lake Crabtree County Park*

(part of the Cary greenway system) on top of the dam; the dam, built in 1987, is part of the Crabtree Watershed Project to create a drainage area of 33,128 acres. The views up the lake are scenic. At 1.2 miles, you will reach a signpost for the trail. At 1.3 miles is a sandy beach area on the right with excellent seats for watching sunsets. You will pass the grassy overflow area, go through a gate, and reach an observation deck for scenic views of the lake at 1.5 miles. At 1.6 miles on the left are an emergency phone and access up the hill to an IBM building, part of Research Triangle Park. Watch for a sudden right turn leaving the paved trail at 1.8 miles; there may be a white blaze instead of blue. (*Black Creek Trail* continues upstream and underneath Weston Parkway on its meandering route to exit at West Dynasty Drive, off North Harrison Avenue; see the section on Cary in chapter 4.)

Rock-hop Black Creek and begin to ascend and descend along the south edge of the lake. You will follow a narrow treadway in and out of coves and pass areas close to the lake, where you will see large hardwoods, with buckeye (a species found in alluvial woods and swamp forests), lavender monarda, and false foxglove. You will cross a wet area at 2.6 miles, enter an old road with a thin passage through grasses and shrubs, and use cement footing for a passage through a swamp at 3.2 miles. Here are cattail, willow, and a cacophony of frogs. You will reach Evans Road at 3.4 miles and walk on a narrow trail at the base of the road shoulder, then cross a steel arched footbridge over Crabtree Creek at 3.6 miles and turn right; there may not be signs or blazes to indicate the direction. Stay right on an old road; you will perhaps see blue blazes near the lake. You will pass through a swampy area to exit at Aviation Parkway near an undeveloped parking area at 4.6 miles. Turn right across the causeway and reenter the forest at the edge of the shoulder railing at 5 miles. Poison ivy is prominent in the woods. You will enter a field of tall grasses and shrubs (these are wet after rains), then approach a manicured lawn of the park. Complete the loop at the *Old Beech Nature Trail* parking lot at 5.4 miles.

*Shelley Lake Trail at Shelley-Sertoma Park, part of Raleigh's greenway system*

# Chapter 4

# TRAILS IN MUNICIPAL PARKS
# AND RECREATION AREAS

More than 135 cities and towns in North Carolina have departments of parks and recreation. Some towns whose boundaries join have formed joint departments, and other cities have teamed with their counties for cooperative services. A few cities are moving swiftly with long-range master plans for greenway systems that will not only serve the inner city but connect with other cities and into the counties. An example is the Raleigh/Durham/Chapel Hill/Cary/Research Triangle greenway plan, supported by a citizens' group, the Triangle Greenways Council. Winston-Salem has a plan to connect with other towns in Forsyth County. Other communities with plans are Charlotte/Mecklenburg County and High Point/Jamestown/Greensboro/Guilford County.

According to 1994–95 figures compiled by city planning departments and chambers of commerce, Raleigh led the state with its parks and recreation budget of $18.6 million and its per-resident spending of $78. The city of Durham budgeted $7.2 million ($49 per resident); Cary budgeted $4.1 million ($68 per resident); and Chapel Hill budgeted $2.4 million ($58 per resident).

Urban trails are usually used for walking, jogging, biking, and in-line skating. They frequently follow streams, city utility routes, nonmotorized roads, recreational parks, and historic areas. Urban trails provide opportunities for appreciating cities' heritage and culture at a relaxed pace, for meeting neighbors, and for physical and spiritual health. Urban walking clubs are growing in popularity, and books and magazines on urban trails are increasing; examples are *Walking* magazine and the book *City Safaris*, by Carolyn Shaffer.

"Trails for day use must be developed in and near urban areas," stated the National Park Service in 1986 when it was developing a national trails system plan. On the following pages are examples of diverse trails whose treadways are city soil, asphalt, brick, and cement. They lead into history and remind us that urban trails are heritage trails.

## BURLINGTON
### Alamance County

The Burlington Recreation and Parks Department and the Burlington Women's Club sponsor Town and Country Nature Park, which offers the easy, 1.5-mile *Town and Country Nature Trail*.

Access to the park is from I-85/40 and NC-87 (exit 147); drive north on South Main Street in Graham. Turn right on NC-49, follow it to US-70 (Church Street), and turn left. Go 0.9 mile and turn right on McKinney Street. After 0.3 mile, turn right on Berkley Road; go 0.2 mile to Regent Park Lane. Park at the end of the street.

Follow the trail signs west on a well-graded path through oak, birch, Virginia pine, black willow, and wildflowers; picnic tables are located at intervals along the trail. You will cross bridges at 0.3 mile and 0.7 mile. You will pass the south side of the Haw River at 0.9 mile. Side trails go up and down the river. (USGS map: Burlington)

*Address:* Recreation and Parks Department, Box 1358, Burlington, NC 27215 (919-226-7371)

## CARRBORO
### Orange County

On the west edge of Carrboro is Carrboro Community Park, a large, modern, well-landscaped facility that would be the pride of any town this size. It offers three lighted ball fields, tennis courts, a playground, a

*Wildlife feeder near Nature Trail in Carrboro Community Park*

picnic area and shelter, and a lake trimmed with the 0.4-mile *Nature Trail* and a forest of oak, beech, maple, pine, and sweet gum. The area is home to duck, goose, squirrel, and songbirds. An easy access is at the first parking place after entering the park.

*Address and Access:* Carrboro Parks and Recreation Department, 301 West Main Street (P.O. Box 829), Carrboro, NC 27510 (919-968-7702). Access from Carrboro Plaza Shopping Center (and the junction of NC-54 Bypass and West Main Street) is 0.7 mile west on NC-54; the park is on the right.

# CARY
## Wake County

The Cary greenway system, begun in 1980, continues to expand within the town limits and to connect with greenways elsewhere in the county. Parks and trail systems are dispersed throughout the area; the greenways frequently follow streams. Examples of greenway diversity are a 7-mile trail system in Fred G. Bond Metro Park and the 0.4-mile *Higgins Trail*, which runs along Swift Creek between Danfort Drive (a crescent off West Chatham Street) to the north and West Maynard Road to the south. Unless otherwise marked at the trailheads, all trails are for walkers and bikers. Paved trails are also open to skaters. Camping is not allowed on any of the trails.

*Black Creek Trail* is an exceptionally scenic 2.5-mile asphalt linear trail that runs from Lake Crabtree County Park on the north to West Dynasty Drive (0.1 mile off North Harrison Avenue) on the south. Access to its northern trailhead is off Weston Parkway on Old Reedy Creek Road; it is 1.3 miles to a gate at Lake Crabtree Dam, on the left. From here, the trail runs conjunctively with *Lake Crabtree Trail* for 1 mile. At 0.5 mile is a sandy beach at the lake. Seats are arranged to provide rest, to watch the birds and sunsets, and to listen to the lake lapping the shoreline. There is an observation deck on the right at 0.7 mile, followed by an emergency telephone on the left at 0.8 mile. At 1 mile, the trail divides. *Lake Crabtree Trail* turns sharply right for a rock-hop over Black Creek to a dirt path (see the section on Wake County in chapter 3). *Black Creek Trail* continues ahead under Weston Parkway and later under Cary Parkway. The trail parallels the creek through a hardwood forest of elm, poplar, oak, and black walnut and among wildflowers

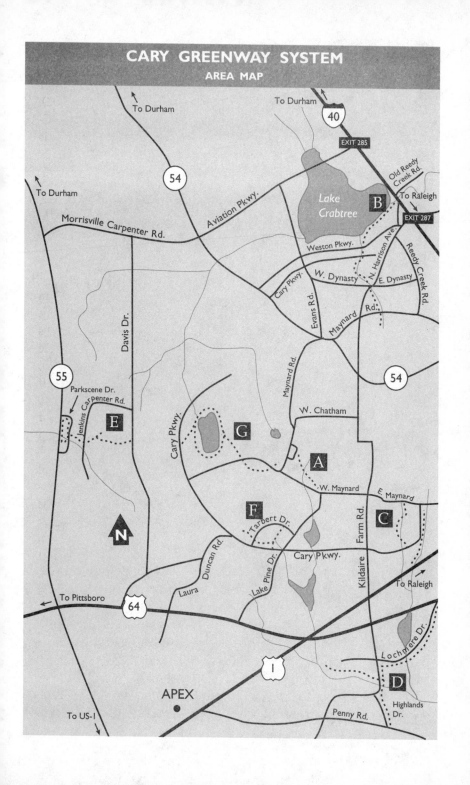

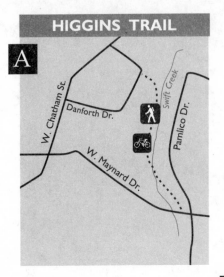

## HIGGINS TRAIL

W. Chatham St.
Danforth Dr.
Swift Creek
Pamlico Dr.
W. Maynard Dr.

**A**

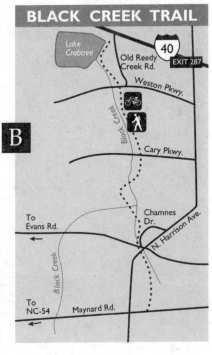

## BLACK CREEK TRAIL

Lake Crabtree
40 EXIT 287
Old Reedy Creek Rd.
Weston Pkwy.
Black Creek
Cary Pkwy.
Chamnes Dr.
N. Harrison Ave.
To Evans Rd.
Black Creek
To NC-54
Maynard Rd.

**B**

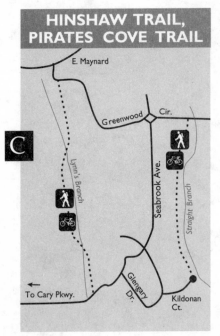

## HINSHAW TRAIL, PIRATES COVE TRAIL

E. Maynard
Greenwood Cir.
Lynn's Branch
Seabrook Ave.
Straight Branch
To Cary Pkwy.
Glengary Dr.
Kildonan Ct.

**C**

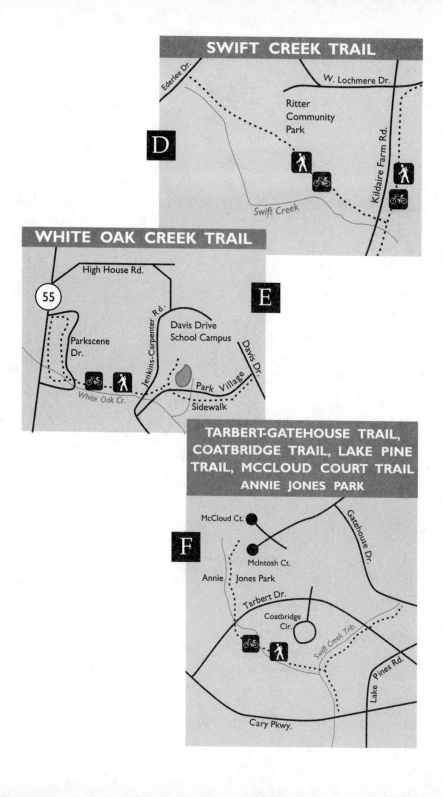

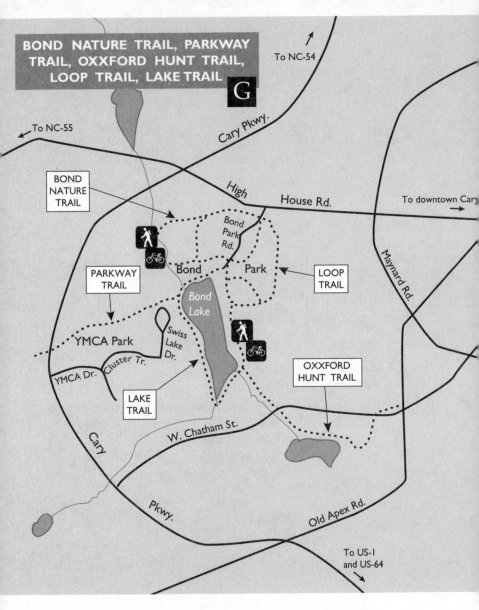

BOND NATURE TRAIL, PARKWAY TRAIL, OXXFORD HUNT TRAIL, LOOP TRAIL, LAKE TRAIL

G

To NC-54

To NC-55

Cary Pkwy.

BOND NATURE TRAIL

High House Rd.

To downtown Cary

Bond Park Rd.

Bond Park

PARKWAY TRAIL

LOOP TRAIL

Bond Lake

Maynard Rd.

YMCA Park

Swiss Lake Dr.

Cluster Tr.

YMCA Dr.

OXXFORD HUNT TRAIL

LAKE TRAIL

Cary

W. Chatham St.

Pkwy.

Old Apex Rd.

To US-1 and US-64

such as cardinal flower and jewelweed. It leaves Black Creek and veers left up a tributary before crossing the last creek bridge at 2.4 miles.

At McDonald Woods Park is the 0.8-mile *Hinshaw Trail*. Access is off Cary Parkway; follow Seabrook Avenue for 0.35 mile to the streetside parking on the right. At the park sign are steps for a descent to a playground, a grassy meadow, and a service road leading 0.2 mile to a gate.

Across the street from the park sign is the asphalt trail. It weaves through a hardwood forest that includes elm, poplar, beech, oak, and hickory to parallel Lynn's Branch, a tributary of Lochmere Lake. The trail's northern terminus is at the junction of Southeast Maynard Road and Greenwood Circle at the parking lot of the Cary Church of Christ.

Near McDonald Woods Park is the 0.6-mile *Pirates Cove Trail*, also a north-south greenway. Its northern access is off Seabrook Avenue on Greenwood Circle; go east 0.1 mile to where the street dead-ends. Its southern trailhead is the dead end of Kildonan Court, which is off the crescent-shaped Glengary Drive (which is in turn off Seabrook Avenue); this access is between McDonald Woods Park and Glenwood Circle. The trail parallels Straight Branch; its treadway is gravel in a hardwood forest. Be alert to fenced-in dogs that may lunge at pedestrians.

*Swift Creek Trail* is unique not because of its plant life or history but because of the composition of its treadway. The wide, smooth trail looks like asphalt, but as part of the Swift Creek Recycled Greenway it contains ash from coal-powered electricity-generating plants, recycled asphalt, rubber tires, roof shingles, and plastics. Perfectly landscaped and offering descriptive signs, the 0.8-mile trail crosses three bridges and runs from Regency Parkway on the west to Kildaire Farm Road on the east; there is a place to park in the center of the route at Ritter Community Park. Access from Kildaire Farm Road is 0.2 mile west on West Lochmere Drive; access is to the left. The trail goes under the Kildaire Farm Road bridge to a T junction. A right turn leads across a footbridge over Swift Creek to connect with the hike/bike trails in the Loch Highland residential development. A left turn connects with a trail at Lochmere Golf Club, where the route parallels Kildaire Farm Road to Lochmere Drive, leading right (east) for 2.5 miles in serpentine fashion to Cary Parkway. (The trail around Lochmere Lake has a No Trespassing sign; usage is for Lochmere residents only.)

A greenway called *White Oak Creek* is in progress for the western area of the city. Access will be from Davis Drive along Park Village Drive. The greenway will connect with a trail near a lake and lead to Davis Drive School; the route will continue downstream to junction with a private greenway (open to the public) between NC-55 and Parkscene Drive.

Below are two parks offering a network of trails.

*Address:* Cary Greenways, 318 North Academy Street (Box 8005), Cary, NC 27512 (919-469-4360)

*Swift Creek Trail, part of Cary's greenway system*

## Annie Jones Park

Located in the southwest part of the city, Annie Jones Park serves a residential area; it offers the Scottish Hills swimming pool, a playground, tennis courts, and a lighted athletic field. Nearby is a small tributary of Swift Creek shaded by young and mature sweet and black gum, maple, poplar, and loblolly pine over ferns and spicebush. To access the park, go three blocks north on Lake Pine Road from the junction with Cary Parkway, turn left (west) on Tarbert Drive, and drive 0.5 mile to a parking lot on the right.

From the park, follow the 0.2-mile *McCloud Court Trail* (part asphalt and gravel) upstream to McCloud Court; backtrack. Downstream is the 0.5-mile *Coatbridge Trail* (natural treadway and gravel), which makes a horseshoe shape in returning to Tarbert Drive between Wishaw Court, to the right (east), and Brodick Court, to the left (west). Across Tarbert Drive is the 0.2-mile, asphalt *Tarbert-Gatehouse Trail*, which passes a playground and ends at Gatehouse Drive; backtrack. On the horseshoe curve of *Coatbridge Trail* is a side trail, the 0.2-mile *Lake Pine Trail*, which continues downstream to the corner of Cary Parkway and Lake Pine Road diagonally opposite a minimart.

## Fred G. Bond Metro Park

On the west side of Cary is Wake County's largest municipal park, the 360-acre Fred G. Bond Metro Park, named in honor of a former Cary mayor. A 42-acre lake offers fishing, boating, and boat rentals. Swimming, wading, and camping are not allowed. Designed to preserve the environment, the park's recreation areas are separated within the forest. There are four lighted athletic fields, a playground, and two picnic shelters, one large enough to accommodate 200 people. The Sertoma Amphitheatre is arranged on a natural slope to seat an audience of more than 350. A color-coded network of trails for hikers and bikers provides multiple loops, described below.

For guided nature tours throughout the year, call 919-387-5980; for reserving the athletic facilities, call 919-469-4062; for reserving picnic shelters, call 919-460-4965.

*Access:* From downtown, go west on Old Apex Road to High House

Road; turn left off High House Road at the park entrance. From the south, follow Cary Parkway off US-1 to High House Road; turn right, then right again at the park entrance.

**Lake Trail** *(2.5 miles)*
**Loop Trail** *(2 miles)*
**Bond Nature Trail** *(0.5 mile)*
**Parkway Trail** *(0.8 mile)*
**Oxxford Hunt Trail** *(1.5 miles)*

*Length and Difficulty:* 7.3 miles combined, easy

*Trailheads and Description:* The trailheads are accessible from any of the parking areas, because they are all connected. None of the trails is paved. The trail system is designed to provide short loop walks or longer combinations. The linear trails (*Parkway Trail* and *Oxxford Hunt Trail*) can be backtracked, or a second vehicle may be used.

One possible loop arrangement is to begin at the parking area near field #1. Enter the woods at par exercise #5 on the physical-fitness course, which may be yellow-blazed; at this point, the physical-fitness course runs right and left with the red-blazed *Loop Trail*. Turn left; after 0.2 mile, you will cross the park's entrance road. At 0.4 mile, you will join *Bond Nature Trail*, which has markers about a variety of plants, including blackjack oak (*Quercus marilandica*), whose wood is used commercially for charcoal. You will cross a paved road (which leads to the right to the Parkway Athletic Complex) at 0.6 mile. At 0.8 mile, you will come out of the woods to a field at the base of the dam; stay left until the trail markers show a right turn. You will reach a junction with the blue-blazed *Lake Trail*, right and left, at 1.1 miles. (The red-blazed *Loop Trail* and the green-blazed *Bond Nature Trail* go left.) Turn right on *Lake Trail* across the dam; this is one of the most scenic views on the hike. To the right at the other end of the dam are steps that descend to the white-blazed *Parkway Trail*. (*Parkway Trail* leads downstream, crosses under Cary Parkway, and ends in a private greenway open to the public.) Turn left and continue around the lake. For the next 1.2 miles, the trail dips into ravines and passes over bridges and boardwalks, sometimes close to the lakeshore. On the hillside slope, it meanders into the backyards of residents, who may watch you pass by their azalea beds and lawn decks. You will cross a footbridge over a stream at 2.6 miles and junction with the white-blazed *Oxxford Hunt Trail* near another bridge. (*Oxxford Hunt Trail* leads 1.5 miles upstream and across West Chatham Street to a private greenway open to public use.) Continue left on a service road. At 2.9 miles, you will rejoin the yellow and red markers to the right and left. Turn right; you will notice par exercise #17. You will pass athletic fields #3 and #2 and return to par exercise #5, the point of origin (left), at 3.4 miles. (USGS map: Cary)

---

## CHAPEL HILL
### Orange County

The Chapel Hill Parks and Recreation Department maintains 13 park areas, two of which have nature trails.

For access to Umstead Park, turn west off Airport Road (NC-86) at Umstead Drive between downtown and the airport. *Umstead Park Nature Trail* is an easy, 1.1-mile route from the parking lot. Follow it across a bridge and turn right or left. If you turn right, connecting trails (some from private homes) come in near the athletic facilities. You will pass large sycamore trees beside the stream. To hike the 0.4-mile *Tanyard Branch Trail*, locate the Umstead Recreation Center from the parking lot. Walk right of the building and along the stream to wooden steps that lead to Caldwell Street. To hike another 0.2 mile, walk along Mitchell Lane to Hargraves Community Center.

To reach Cedar Falls Park, turn east off NC-86 at Weaver Dairy Road (SR-1733) north of the airport. The 0.7-mile, red-blazed *Cedar Falls Park Trail* leaves the parking lot through hardwoods around the tennis court. At 0.5 mile, you will pass the ruins of an old homestead; return.

The remaining trails are part of the Chapel Hill greenway system.

*Address:* Parks and Recreation Department, 306 North Columbia Street, Chapel Hill, NC 27514 (919-968-2700)

### Battle Branch Trail

*Length and Difficulty:* 1.6 miles, easy to moderate

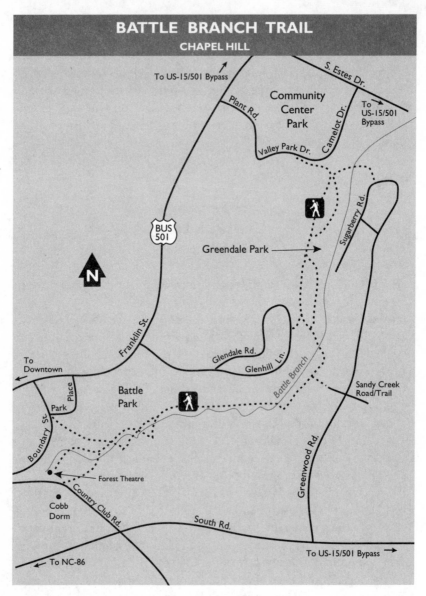

## BATTLE BRANCH TRAIL
### CHAPEL HILL

To US-15/501 Bypass

S. Estes Dr.

Community
Center
Park

Plant Rd.

Camelot Dr.

To
US-15/501
Bypass

Valley Park Dr.

BUS
501

Sugarberry Rd.

Greendale Park

N

Franklin St.

Glendale Rd.

Glenhill Ln.

Battle Branch

To
Downtown

Park Place

Battle
Park

Sandy Creek
Road/Trail

Boundary St.

Greenwood Rd.

Forest Theatre

Cobb
Dorm

Country Club Rd.

South Rd.

To NC-86

To US-15/501 Bypass

*Trailheads and Description:* The western trailhead is at Country Club Road at the University of North Carolina at Chapel Hill; there is no parking except a pull-off at picnic tables. The northeastern trailhead is at Sugarberry Road; parking is streetside only. Parking may be more practical at the Community Center Park parking area, located off East Franklin Street on Plant Road.

*Bicycles are allowed on Durham's North/South Greenway*

If beginning from the west (across the street from Cobb dormitory), descend by the Forest Theatre to Battle Branch. After 0.2 mile, you will reach a junction on the left with the corner of Boundary Street and Park Place. The rocky, rooty double trails—one following a city waste-system road and the other a pathway—crisscross each other and a stream. Towering loblolly pine, oak, and poplar are the principal trees; some of them are entangled with wisteria. Ground beds of ivy and ferns provide diversity in the subcanopy. At 0.5 mile is a steep bluff. At 0.7 mile is a junction with access on the right to *Sandy Creek Trail* and Greenwood Road. You will cross a branch bridge at 1 mile near an access (left) to Glendale Road. A number of boardwalks, steps, and bridges follow; the path stays close to the stream, and a city service road parallels it on a higher contour. At 1.5 miles, the trail forks. A left turn leads to Valley Park Drive; another left turn after 0.2 mile accesses Community Center Park. The right fork crosses a boardwalk among honey locust and privet to ascend steps at Sugarberry Road at 1.6 miles. (USGS map: Chapel Hill)

## Bolin Creek Trail

*Length and Difficulty:* 1.6 miles round-trip, easy

*Trailhead and Description:* To access from downtown Chapel Hill, turn north off East Franklin Street onto Hillsborough Street and drive 0.5 mile to a right turn on Bolinwood Drive; parking is allowed only on the south side of the street near the Bolin Creek bridge.

The elegantly landscaped, wide asphalt greenway is phase 1 along the creek. Plant life on the trail includes redbud, mullen, autumn olive, oak, and loblolly pine. If you are walking upstream first, it is 0.2 mile to Airport Road. Backtrack and continue downstream to the seats at the trail's end. Backtrack to the starting point. (USGS map: Chapel Hill)

# DURHAM
### Durham County

The Durham Parks and Recreation Department maintains more than

62 developed parks and seven undeveloped parks. Two of the parks have a network of trails; they are described below. The Durham Open Space and Trails Commission has master plans for nearly 170 miles of trails in the city and county. One plan is for the North/South Greenway. Completed on the route are *Rock Quarry Trail* and *South Ellerbee Creek Trail*, for a distance of 2.3 miles. From *Rock Quarry Trail*, plans are to extend the greenway northwest to Whippowill Park, a distance of about 2 miles. An extension south from Dacian Street is planned for a distance of about 1.5 miles. It will connect with the proposed 15- to 20-mile *American Tobacco Trail*, a former railroad property of the Norfolk Southern Corporation.

*Address:* Director, Parks and Recreation Department, 101 City Hall Plaza, Durham, NC 27701 (919-560-4355).

## West Point on Eno

This 373-acre city park emphasizes the history and the recreation potential of the West Point Mill community, which existed from 1778 to 1942. Restored and reconstructed are the McCown-Mangum farmhouse, mill, blacksmith shop, and gardens. The Hugh Mangum Museum of Photography is also on the property. The park offers picnicking, fishing, rafting, canoeing, and hiking. Camping and swimming are not allowed. The park is supported by Friends of West Point, Inc., 5101 Roxboro Road, Durham, NC 27704 (919-471-1623). (USGS map: Durham NW)

**Buffalo Trail** *(0.5 mile)*
**South Eno River Trail** *(1.7 miles)*
**North Eno River Trail** *(1.7 miles)*

*Length and Difficulty:* 3.9 miles combined, easy to moderate

*Trailheads and Description:* From I-85 in Durham, take US-501 Bypass (North Duke Street) north for 3.4 miles and turn left into the park; the turn is across the road from the Riverview Shopping Center. Follow the park road to a small parking area on the right at the trail signboard, located across the road from the picnic shelter and restrooms.

*Buffalo Trail* ascends a ridge and descends to a junction with *South Eno River Trail* after 0.5 mile. If you are taking *South Eno River Trail*, walk down the park road to the mill. Cross the millrace bridge and turn left

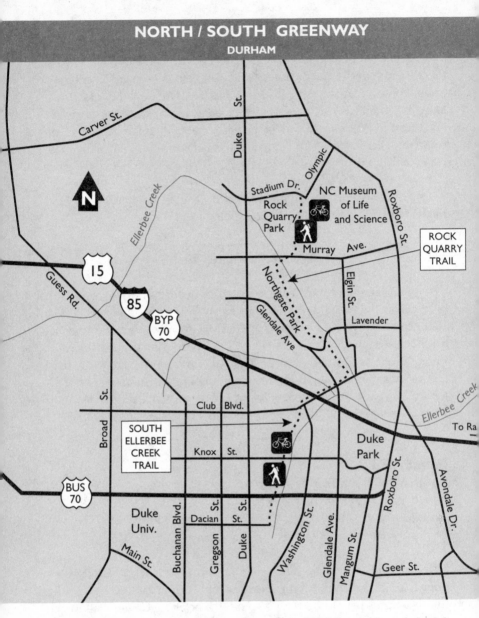

Carver St.

Duke St.

N

Ellerbee Creek

Stadium Dr.

Olympic

Rock Quarry Park

NC Museum of Life and Science

Murray Ave.

Roxboro St.

15

Guess Rd.

85

BYP 70

Northgate Park

Glendale Ave

Elgin St.

Lavender

Broad St.

Club Blvd.

Ellerbee Creek

To Ra

SOUTH ELLERBEE CREEK TRAIL

Knox St.

Duke Park

BUS 70

Duke Univ.

Main St.

Buchanan Blvd.

Dacian St.

Gregson St.

Duke St.

Washington St.

Glendale Ave.

Mangum St.

Roxboro St.

Avondale Dr.

Geer St.

to the dam. You will ascend in a forest of hardwoods and laurel. At 0.2 mile and 0.3 mile are spur trails leading left to *Buffalo Trail*. At 0.6 mile, you will junction with *Buffalo Trail*, on the left. Turn right and rock-hop a stream. You will arrive at Sennett Hole (the site of the first gristmill on the river) and its scenic views at 0.7 mile. Continue upriver on rocky ledges among laurel, rhododendron, yellow root, trillium, spring beauty, wild ginger, river birch, and sycamore. At 1.7 miles, you will reach Guess Road. You can either backtrack or cross the bridge and locate an old road to the right that leads to *North Eno River Trail,* a footpath downriver. Follow the north bank to a cement high-water bridge below the dam. Cross the bridge to the mill and return to the point of origin at 1.7 miles.

---

## Rock Quarry Park and Northgate Park

**Rock Quarry Trail** *(1.2 miles)*
**South Ellerbee Creek Trail** *(0.9 mile)*

*Length and Difficulty:* 2.3 miles combined, easy

*Trailheads and Description:* (These trails are part of the city's North/South Greenway.) The parking area for Rock Quarry Park is on Stadium Drive 0.3 mile from North Duke Street and 0.9 mile from I-85. The park has athletic fields and tennis courts.

From the entrance to the ball field, follow the *Rock Quarry Trail* sign beside the restrooms and into the forest on a broad asphalt bike/hike trail. At 0.2 mile, you will pass left of a Vietnam War memorial. Here are meditation benches. One of the statements carved in the marble reads, "For those who fought for it, freedom has a flavor the protected will never know." You will pass the Edison Johnson Recreation Center and the North Carolina Museum of Life and Science on the sidewalk to Murray Street. Cross the street, turn right, and continue over the Ellerbee Creek bridge to an immediate left at the trail sign to enter Northgate Park.

You will follow an asphalt trail across a meadow. After 125 yards is a replica of a brontosaurus. You will then enter a shady area among large oak and pine and pass around the edge of a lighted Jaycee ball field in Northgate Park at 0.8 mile. Continue on the trail through elm, maple, and evergreens and cross Lavender Avenue. Willow, oak, ash, sycamore, and poplar tower over a peaceful lawn with squirrel and songbirds. Across a footbridge to the left are a playground, a picnic shelter, and parking areas. You will arrive at West Club Boulevard, the south end of *Rock Quarry Trail,* and the beginning of *South Ellerbee Creek Trail* at 1.2

miles. Turn right on the sidewalk, cross Glendale Avenue, pass Club Boulevard Elementary School, and go under US-15/70 Bypass. At the Washington Street traffic light, cross to the southwest corner of the intersection at 1.6 miles. You will descend on a wide, recently constructed greenway through a forest with tall trees and large, swinging grapevines. The greenway is like a golden path of opportunity for neighbors to visit each other on a tranquil street; children can walk or ride their bikes from near the crowded heart of the city north to a museum, a swimming pool, athletic fields, and acres of green grass. The disabled can use wheelchairs for a touch with nature. At 1.7 miles, you will pass the manicured back lawns of private homes. You will cross Knox Street at 1.9 miles, then cross an arched wood and steel bridge near banks of wild roses. You will cross Green Street and Markham Street and pass under a power line to complete the trail at the end of Dacian Street at 2.3 miles. (USGS map: Durham NW)

## GOLDSBORO
### Wayne County

*Stoney Creek Trail* begins at Quail Park and will eventually extend to the Neuse River. (See page 84 for map.) To approach Quail Park, turn off US-70/13 Bypass at Wayne Memorial Drive and go south to the first street on the left, Newton Drive. Turn left again on Quail Drive to reach the park. (See map on page 89, which also shows *Wayne County Trail*, a section of the *Mountains-to-Sea Trail* described on page 48 and in Chapter 6.)

Walk past the picnic shelter to Stoney Creek and turn downstream through the Kemp Greenway; the trail blazes may be yellow or white. Plant life includes tall river birch, poplar, maple, laurel oak, ironweed, cardinal flower, dayflower, beauty-bush, and sensitive fern. This trail is also good for bird-watching. Cross Royal Street and go under the railroad trestle at 0.3 mile. At 1.1 miles, you will cross Ash Street and enter Stoney Creek Park. At 1.8 miles, you will cross Elm Street; on the left is an entrance gate to Seymour Johnson Air Force Base. Go 130 yards to a dead-end street where there is parking space. *Wayne County Trail* continues 2.3 miles to Slocumb Street Extension and the entrance to Seymour Johnson Air Base on the left. (USGS maps: Goldsboro NE, Goldsboro SE)

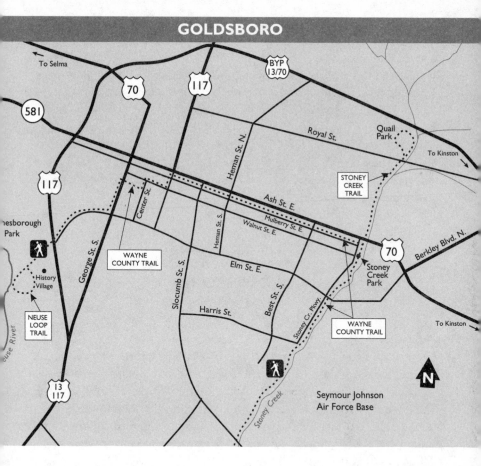

*Address:* Director, Parks and Recreation Department, Drawer A, Goldsboro, NC 27530 (919-734-9397)

## HENDERSON

### Vance County

Fox Pond Park offers lighted tennis courts, a picnic area with shelters, a playground, a baseball field, fishing, and trails. No swimming is allowed. The park is open all year.

From the parking lot near the tennis courts, begin the 1.4-mile *Fox Pond Trail* on the east side of the lake; go counterclockwise. You will cross a floating bridge at the lake's headwaters at 0.5 mile. You will then cross a service road near a cement bunker at 0.9 mile, cross the stream on a swinging bridge near the dam at 1.3 miles, and return to the parking lot. East of the parking lot is the 0.6-mile *Conoconors Trail*, which loops through sweet gum and poplar trees around the tennis courts. *Quarry Trail* and *Sutton's Island Trail* are short loops of 0.2 mile each in the recreation area.

*Address and Access:* Director, Recreation and Parks Department, Box 1556, Henderson, NC 27536 (919-492-6111). Access is from NC-39, 0.4 mile east of US-1 Bypass; turn on Huff Road (SR-1533) and go 0.5 mile to the park, on the left.

## LOUISBURG
### Franklin County

The Franklin County Soil and Water Conservation District and the town of Louisburg have created the 15-acre Fox Creek Nature Lab at the confluence of the Tar River and Fox Creek. The lab has four stations for testing water quality and studying wildlife, wetlands, and forestry. The 0.5-mile *Fox Creek Nature Trail* makes an infinity loop under exceptionally old oak, by a swamp of cypress, and through beds of ferns and wildflowers. Visitation is by appointment; tour guides are available. (USGS map: Louisburg)

*Address and Access:* Soil and Water Conservation District, 101 South Bickett Boulevard, Suite B, Louisburg, NC 27549 (919-496-3137). From the junction of US-401 and NC-56 (East Nash Street), go east on NC-56 for 0.4 mile and turn right on a narrow road to the wastewater treatment plant.

## RALEIGH
### Wake County

The Raleigh Parks and Recreation Department maintains a comprehensive system of 131 parks and recreation areas. Part of its program is the Capital City Greenway, a model development for municipal planning consisting of 245 parcels of land. The greenway system was begun in 1974 when the city responded to rapid urbanization that threatened its natural beauty. The master plan provides a system of wide trails in their natural state for recreational activities such as walking, jogging, hiking, fishing, picnicking, bicycling, and nature study. The trails mainly follow floodplains or utility areas associated with the city's three major streams—the Neuse River and Crabtree and Walnut Creeks—and their tributaries.

Two greenway trails unrelated to those covered below are *Gardner Street Trail* and *Marsh Creek Trail*.

At the Rose Garden and Raleigh Little Theatre, *Gardner Street Trail* begins at the corner of Gardner and Everette Streets at the greenway sign; the park entrance is on Gardner Street. You will descend and pass left of a restroom and a basketball court. Cross Kilgore Street and follow the sidewalk briefly. After crossing Van Dyke Avenue, turn left on Fairall Drive, a gravel road shaded by tall poplar, oak, and loblolly pine. At 0.6 mile, you will enter a forest. You will arrive at Jaycee Park on Wade Avenue at 0.8 mile.

The paved, 0.4-mile *Marsh Creek Trail* is at Brentwood Park, located at the end of Vinson Court. The wide trail follows Marsh Creek from Ingram Drive to a footbridge over the stream at the end of Glenraven Drive.

Because the majority of the trails covered below are paved, they can be used by the physically handicapped. Some of the shorter connecting trails are described in greenway groups. The five longest trails—*Lake Johnson, Lake Lynn, Loblolly, Neuse River*, and *Shelley Lake Trails*—are described separately. A Raleigh greenway map is helpful for locating trailheads.

*Address:* Director, Parks and Recreation Department, Box 590, Raleigh, NC 27602 (919-890-3285)

## Crabtree Greenway Area

On the Crabtree Creek floodplain and part of the Crabtree Creek greenway project are *Alleghany, Lassiter's Mill, Fallon Creek*, and *Buckeye Trails*. They will eventually connect with each other for a route up Lead Mine Creek to the Shelley Lake trails.

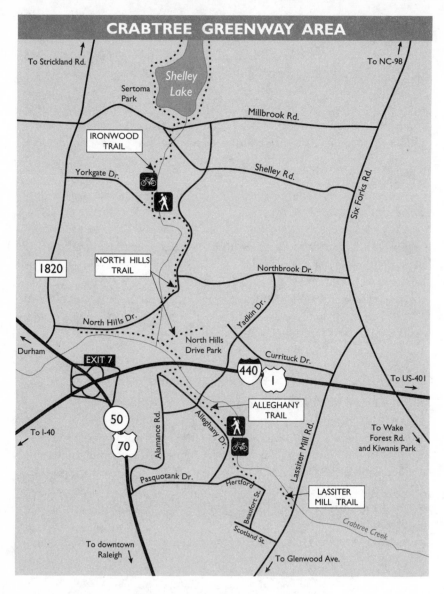

# CRABTREE GREENWAY AREA

To Strickland Rd.

To NC-98

*Shelley Lake*

Sertoma Park

Millbrook Rd.

IRONWOOD TRAIL

Yorkgate Dr.

Shelley Rd.

Six Forks Rd.

NORTH HILLS TRAIL

Northbrook Dr.

1820

North Hills Dr.

Yadkin Dr.

Durham

North Hills Drive Park

EXIT 7

440  I

Currituck Dr.

To US-401

50

ALLEGHANY TRAIL

To I-40

70

Alamance Rd.

Alleghany Dr.

To Wake Forest Rd. and Kiwanis Park

Lassiter Mill Rd.

Pasquotank Dr.

Hertford

LASSITER MILL TRAIL

*Crabtree Creek*

Beaufort St.

Scotland St.

To downtown Raleigh

To Glenwood Ave.

   The paved, 0.4-mile *Alleghany Trail* follows Crabtree Creek in a forest of tall poplar, willow oak, and loblolly pine. It passes under the Yadkin Drive bridge (southeast) and the I-440 bridge (northwest). To access the trail, park on the side of Alleghany Drive near its junction with Alamance Drive or Buncombe Street; the northern trailhead may also be accessed from *North Hills Trail*.

*North Hills Trail* is a unique trio of fascinating asphalt routes, two of which may also be called *Ironwood Trail Extension.* The combined round-trip is 3.1 miles. *North Hills Trail* can be accessed from *Alleghany Trail* off Alleghany Drive or North Hills Park off Currituck Drive, which is off Yadkin Drive. If proceeding from the North Hills Park tennis court parking lot, you will descend steeply to wetlands thick with elm, ash, yellow poplar, lizard's tail, and jewelweed at 0.2 mile. (To the left is *Alleghany Trail,* which leads downstream under the I-440 bridge and over an arched bridge at Crabtree Creek.) To follow *North Hills Trail,* turn right. After 0.1 mile, you will cross a boardwalk over Lead Mine Creek to a fork. To the right, this part of the trail goes 0.3 mile to North Hills Drive. To the left, the trail hugs the bank of Crabtree Creek among tall trees for 0.4 mile to North Hills Drive and a temporary dead end across from a day-care center. Backtrack on all three parts. (See the section on the Shelley Lake trails below.)

The 0.2-mile *Lassiter's Mill Trail* is a paved route from Lassiter Mill Road upstream to the dam where Cornelius Jesse Lassiter operated a 1764 gristmill from 1908 to 1958. To access the trail, park on Old Lassiter Mill Road a few yards from the junction with Lassiter Mill Road.

Two other trails are downstream on the south side of Crabtree Creek. *Fallon Creek Trail,* a paved, 0.3-mile, 21-post interpretive trail, goes through tall elm, ash, poplar, and hackberry. A champion river birch (8.5 feet in girth) is near Crabtree Creek. Understory trees are box elder, hornbeam, holly, and dogwood. To access the trail, park at Kiwanis Park at the end of Noble Street or on Oxford Road 0.1 mile downstream from its junction with Anderson Drive. *Buckeye Trail* is a paved, scenic, meandering 2.4-mile route in a deep forest of tall river birch, poplar, willow oak, and loblolly pine. If parking at the upstream parking area on Crabtree Boulevard, walk 240 yards downstream (east) on the sidewalk and around the curve to the forest entrance. You will pass a picnic area at 0.2 mile, a playground at 1.4 miles, and a maintenance entrance from Crabtree Boulevard at 1.6 miles. On the left at 1.9 miles is an observation deck with a ramp for the handicapped; it is located on a knoll with views of the river. You will descend and at 2.4 miles reach the eastern trailhead parking area, where there is access to Crabtree Park and Milburnie Road off US-64 west of the I-440 junction.

# Walnut Creek Greenway Area

In the Walnut Creek area are *Lake Johnson Trail* (described on page 97) and *Rocky Branch, Little Rock,* and *Dacian Valley Trails.*

*Rocky Branch Trail* is a paved 1.5-mile route. Begin at the Dix Hospital entrance on Umstead Drive at Saunders Street; parking is on the left 140 yards up Umstead Drive from the trailhead, right. You will descend steps and pass through an open meadow with large pecan trees and a picnic area. You will then cross Boylan Avenue at 0.3 mile, enter a forest, exit onto a sidewalk of Western Boulevard, cross Hunt Drive at 0.6 mile, and cross the Rocky Branch bridge. At 1.1 miles, you will cross Bilyeu Street. After 0.1 mile, you will follow an old paved roadway to the corner of Bilyeu Street and Cardinal Gibbons Street near the south side of Cardinal Gibbons High School.

*Little Rock Trail* is a paved 0.7-mile route at Chavis Park; parking is on Chavis Way. From the corner of Lenoir and Chavis Way, you will cross the Garner Branch footbridge, pass two picnic areas, cross Bragg Street at 0.5 mile, and end at McMackin Street. Tall elm, ash, and sycamore shade the trail.

*Dacian Valley Trail* is a 0.3-mile loop beginning at a picnic area at the end of Dacian Road. You will pass through tall hardwoods near Walnut Creek. This trail connects with *Walnut Creek Trail.*

The 1.2-mile *Walnut Creek Trail* is part of the Capital City Greenway system in Raleigh's southeastern section; the system will connect with Lake Johnson to the west and the Neuse River to the east. From New Bern Avenue in the city, access to *Walnut Creek Trail* is 1.2 miles south on Raleigh Boulevard, which merges with Rock Quarry Road. From the south, drive north on Rock Quarry Road from US-40/440, exit 300, for 0.3 mile to the roadside parking on the right. The skillfully constructed nine-foot-wide asphalt trail descends to the side of Walnut Creek and stays on the north side the entire distance. A large, lush marsh on the right at 0.2 mile features lizard's tail, cattail, arrow arum, and a former beaver hutch in the center. Woodpeckers have made homes in some of the dead trees. You will pass under exceptionally tall trees such as loblolly pine, sycamore, river birch, poplar, and oak. Songbirds are prominent. A dense understory of elderberry and privet is in the damp areas. At 0.3 mile is a long boardwalk over Gatling Branch. At 0.4 mile is a side trail to a parking area for the Ralph Campbell Sr. Community Center on Carmen Court. A playground and a basketball court are located at 1 mile. At 1.1 miles is a marsh on the trail's left. The trail ends at the gravel Rose Lane at a bridge over Walnut Creek. (USGS map: Raleigh E)

## Durant Nature Park

This is a former private preserve with an emphasis on children's summer camping and nature study. The Raleigh Parks and Recreation Department continues the nature-study concept with Ranoca North Day Camp in session during June, July, and August. There are Sawmill and Blind Water Lakes, a beaver pond, a swimming dock, a boathouse, a playing field, and a training lodge. (USGS map: Wake Forest)

*Address and Access:* Ranoca North Day Camp, Parks and Recreation Department, Box 590, Raleigh, NC 27602 (919-870-2872). The number for the main office at Pullen Community Center is 919-831-6054. Access from the south is on Greshams Lake Road off US-1. Turn right on Welborn, then right on Spotswood; the park entrance is on the left. Access from the north is west off US-1 on Durant Road for 1.1 miles; turn left at the sign.

**Border Trail** *(1.5 miles)*
**Lakeside Trail** *(1.2 miles)*
**Secret Creek Trail** *(0.5 mile)*

*Length and Difficulty:* 3.7 miles combined round-trip, easy

*Trailheads and Description:* From the northern parking area, enter *Border Trail* from the southwest corner on an old woods road; watch for the signs. Turn right at 0.1 mile. At 0.2 mile, you will go upstream on Reedy Branch among large loblolly pine and yellow poplar by Sheet Rock Falls. You will later leave the stream and enter a preserve of tall trees, running cedar, ferns, wild ginger, and spicebush. You will cross a footbridge over Sim's Branch at 1 mile. At 1.2 miles are a wisteria grove and the remnants of an old homesite. To the left are views of a beaver pond and Blind Water Lake, also called Upper Lake. You will junction with *Lakeside Trail* at 1.5 miles. A right turn for a loop leads around Sawmill Lake for 1.2 miles over the dam, by the bathhouse, and through the forest to a spillway of Blind Water Lake. Backtrack 0.5 mile to the northeast corner

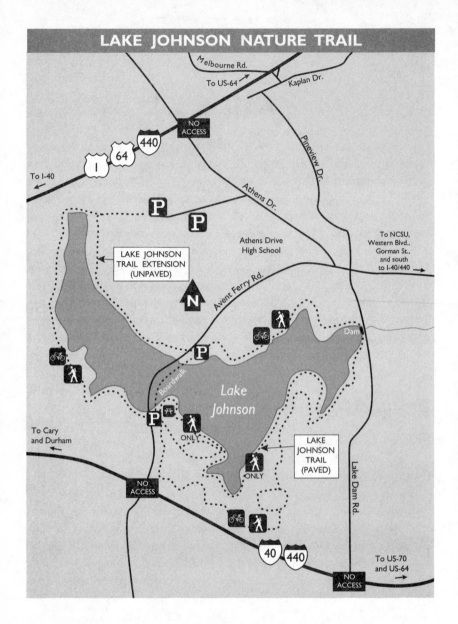

of Sawmill Lake at Sycamore Picnic Shelter to begin *Secret Creek Trail*. You will follow it by a rocky streambed, ferns, elm, and wild petunia. Exit near the totem poles, turn right, and return to the parking area for a total of 3.7 miles.

# Lake Johnson Nature Park

## Lake Johnson Trail

*Length and Difficulty:* 3.6 miles, easy

*Trailhead and Description:* From near the WRAL-TV station and gardens on Western Boulevard, take Avent Ferry Road 3.2 miles and park at the lot on the south side of Lake Johnson (across the causeway).

You will enter a young hardwood forest and reach a picnic shelter; hike counterclockwise. You will cross a small stream and pass a small waterfall at 0.6 mile. You will then wind in and out of coves among tall trees, reach the dam and spillway at 1.6 miles, and cross a bridge over the spillway and the rim of the dam for scenic views. At 1.8 miles, you will junction with a spur trail leading to the right to Lake Dam Road; there is no parking here. Continue left. You will arrive at the picnic and boathouse parking area at Avent Ferry Road at 2.6 miles. Turn left on a high pedestrian/bike bridge that parallels the lake's causeway for a return to complete the loop at 3 miles.

A greenway trail continues across the road from the boat dock at Avent Ferry Road. This wide wood-chip trail passes north of Lake Johnson in a scenic area. After 0.3 mile, bear right. You will ascend to a parking area at 0.6 mile at William Stadium behind Athens Drive High School.

Both of these trails are part of the Walnut Creek greenway system. (USGS map: Raleigh W)

## Richland Creek Area

## Loblolly Trail

*Length and Difficulty:* 6 miles, easy

*Trailhead and Description:* Take the Blue Ridge Road exit from Wade Avenue, go south 0.4 mile to Old Trinity Road, and turn right. Park to the left of gate D at Carter-Finley Stadium.

You will follow a grassy road in a grassy field to the northwest, pass left of a drain pool, and enter the forest at 0.2 mile. Follow the old road.

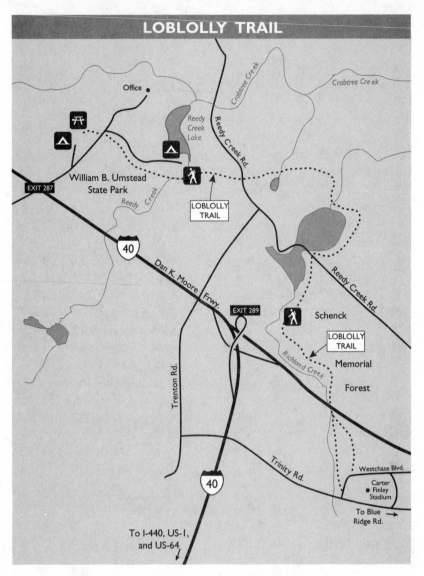

# LOBLOLLY TRAIL

Office

Crabtree Creek

Crabtree Creek

Reedy
Creek
Lake

Reedy Creek Rd.

LOBLOLLY
TRAIL

William B. Umstead
State Park

EXIT 287

Reedy Creek

40

Dan K. Moore Frwy.

EXIT 289

Reedy Creek Rd.

Schenck

LOBLOLLY
TRAIL

Memorial

Forest

Richland Creek

Trenton Rd.

Trinity Rd.

Westchase Blvd.

Carter
● Finley
Stadium

To Blue
Ridge Rd.

40

To I-440, US-1,
and US-64

You will cross a rock ditch at 0.4 mile and confront the base of Wade
Avenue at a small gate at 0.6 mile. Walk through the square cement
culvert under Wade Avenue; wading may be necessary. Proceed downstream among river birch. At 1.3 miles, you will enter the North Carolina State University (NCSU) forest management area of conifers and
broadleaves. At 2.2 miles, you will junction with NCSU's 1.2-mile *Frances
Liles Interpretive Trail* loop, to the right in Schenck Memorial Forest; be-

tween the trail accesses is an NCSU weir gauging station. You will arrive at Reedy Creek Park Road at 2.4 miles. (Wake County Flood Control Lake is to the left; to the right, it is 1.7 miles to Blue Ridge Road.) Turn right. After 150 yards, turn left off the road to an obscure trail entrance near the road-shoulder parking. You will pass through a damp cove and a dry, rocky lakeside among redbud and young hardwoods. At 3 miles, you will enter a fence opening to cross the dam. At the dam's base, cross the creek and veer right to enter the forest at another gate opening at 3.1 miles. You will then pass among young river birch on an old road; turn left at 3.2 miles. You will ascend in an open forest to enter William B. Umstead State Park at 3.3 miles, where the trail becomes blue-blazed. You will cross a horse trail at 3.6 miles, descend to a damp hollow, pass to the right of a pond at 3.8 miles, and cross a park service road at 4.2 miles. After crossing two more small streams that feed Reedy Creek Lake, you will cross a high footbridge over Reedy Creek at 5.1 miles. You will pass under a power line at 5.7 miles, cross Camp Whispering Pines Road, and arrive at the Reedy Creek parking area of William B. Umstead State Park at 6 miles.

Access here is 0.3 mile from I-40. For information on the trails in William B. Umstead State Park, see chapter 2. (USGS maps: Cary, Raleigh W)

## Neuse River Greenway Area

### Neuse River Trail

*Length and Difficulty:* 4 miles, easy

*Trailhead and Description:* This linear trail parallels the Neuse River and goes under US-64 on the east side of the city. To access the trail from the south, drive 0.9 mile east on US-64 from its junction with New Hope Road and turn right on Rogers Lane; after 1.3 miles, turn left into the parking lot. To access the northern trailhead, drive 0.9 mile north on New Hope Road from US-64, turn right on Southall Road, go 0.8 mile, turn right on Castlebrook Drive, go 0.5 mile, and turn right on Abington Lane to the parking lot and the dead-end road.

If entering from the south, you will follow a wide road made from a city waste line. Tall hickory, beech, and loblolly pine are prominent. Birds and butterflies are among the willow, wax myrtle, and wildflowers. At 1.1 miles is a long boardwalk in a wet area inhabited by frogs.

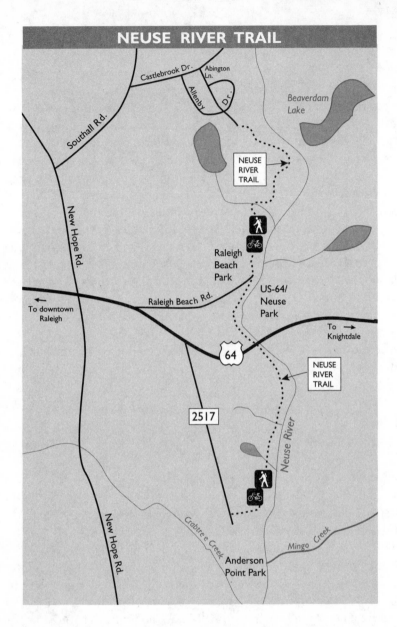

NEUSE RIVER TRAIL

Castlebrook Dr.

Abington Ln.

Allenby Dr.

Southall Rd.

Beaverdam Lake

NEUSE RIVER TRAIL

New Hope Rd.

Raleigh Beach Park

US-64/ Neuse Park

Raleigh Beach Rd.

To downtown Raleigh

To Knightdale

64

NEUSE RIVER TRAIL

2517

Neuse River

New Hope Rd.

Crabtree Creek

Mingo Creek

Anderson Point Park

You will pass under US-64 at 1.5 miles. Turn left at a trail post, then right on Raleigh Beach Road at 2.1 miles. After 0.1 mile, you will turn left, go up a hill for 130 yards, and make a right turn toward the woods. At 2.7 miles are a bridge, a small beaver dam, and a wet area with water hyacinth. You will pass left of a swamp at 3.3 miles. You will then curve away from the river, ascend a rocky area, and exit at the parking lot. You can either backtrack or have a second car waiting for you. (USGS map: Raleigh E)

## Shelley-Sertoma Park

**Shelley Lake Trail** *(2.2 miles)*
**Snelling Branch Trail** *(0.6 mile)*
**Bent Creek Trail** *(1 mile)*
**Sawmill Trail** *(1 mile)*
**Ironwood Trail** *(0.8 mile)*

*Length and Difficulty:* 5.6 miles combined, easy (the round-trip and backtracking distance is 7.4 miles above the dam and 1.6 miles downstream below the dam)

*Trailheads and Description:* From the junction of US-70 and NC-50 at Crabtree Valley Mall, take NC-50 north 0.8 mile to Millbrook Road (SR-1812). Turn right and go 1 mile to Shelley-Sertoma Park, on the left. Another route to the park follows Millbrook Road 1.3 miles from Six Forks Road. Parking is available both at the arts center and below the dam.

If parking below the dam, you will enter the trail near Lead Mine Creek at the junction of *Shelley Lake Trail*, to the left, and *Ironwood Trail*, to the right; *Shelley Lake Trail* is a national recreation trail. Follow the paved trail to the top of the dam and a fork. If following the paved trail from the dam on the grassy east side of the lake, you will cross a boardwalk and enter a forest of sweet gum, oak, and river birch at 0.2 mile. At 0.7 mile is an emergency phone to the right; to the left is an alternate trail to an observation deck near the lake. At 0.8 mile, you will reach a junction with *Snelling Branch Trail*, to the right. (*Snelling Branch Trail* crosses North Hills Drive after 0.3 mile, passes a baseball field to the left and Sanderson High School to the right, and ends at the Optimist Club parking lot at 0.6 mile. Access here is off Northcliff Drive.) Continue on *Shelley Lake Trail* across a small stream with banks of yellow root and shade from river birch and yellow poplar. At 0.9 mile, you will cross a wide bridge over Lead Mine Creek among elm and ironwood. To the right is *Bent Creek Trail*, which parallels Lead Mine Creek on a

*Shelley Lake Trail*
*Photo courtesy of The* News and Observer

wide asphalt route. At 0.1 mile, it goes through a tunnel under North Hill Road, after which a 0.2-mile unpaved alternate side trail veers right. (This side trail follows the rim of the stream through ironwood, dogwood, large poplar, river birch, and spicebush. At the halfway mark on the trail is a scenic bend in the creek at a sand bar. The side trail exits on *Bent Creek Trail* in sight of the Lynn Road bridge.)

If staying on the main route of *Bent Creek Trail*, you will pass through poplar and river birch; Christmas fern is underneath redbud beside the trail. You will go under the Lynn Road bridge, enter a forest of black walnut, poplar, and large grapevine, cross a steel and wood arched bridge over Lead Mine Creek, and junction with *Sawmill Trail*, located on the left at 0.6 mile. (The scenic *Sawmill Trail* is a dirt path for foot travel only. It begins on the east side of Lead Mine Creek but crosses and follows a tributary at 0.4 mile. Along the way are rocks shaped like petrified logs. At 0.7 mile near a boardwalk is a patch of cardinal flower. Other flowers by the stream are yellow root and jack-in-the-pulpit. After the last bridge, the trail enters an open area and ends at Sawmill Road; there is no parking here.)

To complete *Bent Creek Trail*, follow the asphalt route and cross a bridge

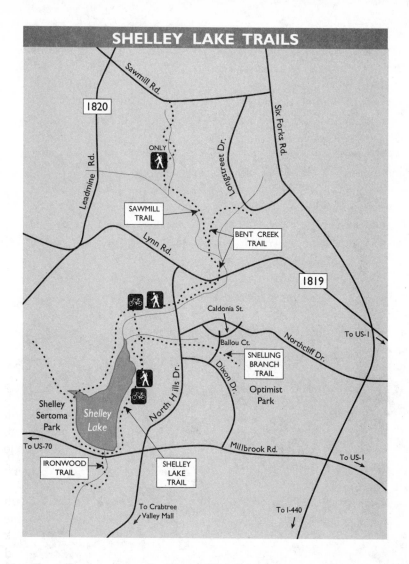

SHELLEY LAKE TRAILS

1820

ONLY

Sawmill Rd.

Leadmine Rd.

Longstreet Dr.

Six Forks Rd.

SAWMILL TRAIL

BENT CREEK TRAIL

Lynn Rd.

1819

Caldonia St.

Ballou Ct.

Northcliff Dr.

To US-1

SNELLING BRANCH TRAIL

Optimist Park

Dixon Dr.

North Hills Dr.

Shelley Sertoma Park

Shelley Lake

To US-70

IRONWOOD TRAIL

SHELLEY LAKE TRAIL

Millbrook Rd.

To US-1

To Crabtree Valley Mall

To I-440

over Bent Creek at 0.8 mile. You will curve left and ascend beside the stream, which has small pools and cascades. Poplar, beech, and tag alder shade the rocky area. Exit at the corner of Longstreet Drive and Bent Creek Drive at 1 mile; curbside parking is available here. Backtrack to *Shelley Lake Trail* to complete its loop.

After returning to *Shelley Lake Trail*, you will reach an emergency telephone and junction with a short asphalt trail leading right to Lakeway Drive at 1.3 miles. You will have views of the lake. At 1.6 miles are a support wall and an observation tower. You will cross a long, high, wide bridge over the lake, a popular and scenic place to feed and watch the ducks and geese and for children to fish. You will pass an access (right) to the arts center and *Lake Park Trail*, a side trail for residents on Rushing Brook Drive. Restrooms and a bathhouse are to the left. Return to the point of origin at 2.2 miles.

*Ironwood Trail* follows Lead Mine Creek downstream from the parking area below Shelely Lake Dam. Go south under the Shelley Road bridge. You will wind through the forest, cross the stream three times, and exit in the 5200 block of North Hills Drive.

The trail will eventually connect downstream with *Ironwood Trail Extension* and lead to North Hills Park and *Alleghany Trail* at the Crabtree Creek confluence. At present, the connection can be made by walking 0.4 mile on the sidewalk of North Hills Drive. (USGS map: Raleigh W)

*Lake Lynn Trail, part of Raleigh's greenway system*

# Lake Lynn and Lake Lynn Park

**Lake Lynn Trail** (*2.1 miles, easy*)
**Lake Lynn Park Trail** (*0.3 mile, easy*)

*Length and Difficulty:* 2.7 miles combined round-trip, easy

*Trailheads and Description:* Access from the west is off US-70 on Lynn Road; drive 1.3 miles to the parking area on the left near the base of the dam. Access from the east is from Crabtree Valley Mall; drive north on NC-50 off US-70 for 2 miles to Lynn Road; turn left and drive 0.8 mile west to the parking lot, on the right. Access from the north is at Lake Lynn Park off Ray Road.

Lake Lynn is fed by Hare Snip Creek and a few smaller tributaries. It is part of the Capital City Greenway system. Like *Shelly Lake Trail* (about 1.5 miles east), the area is frequented by walkers, strollers, joggers, runners, bikers, and a few in-line skaters. Its design also serves the residential neighborhood, where private backyards and the porches of apartments merge into the landscape of the trail so completely that trail users must remember that the swimming pools on the east and west sides of the lake are not for public use.

Although the lake loop is 2.1 miles, *Lake Lynn Park Trail* adds another 0.6-mile back-and-forth route. Branching off from it is a 0.2-mile (0.4-mile round-trip) gravel spur trail to Ray Road. The main loop trail has six boardwalks, the longest of which leads across the marshy north end of the lake, a watery respite for turtle and waterfowl. Every 0.25 mile are distance markers. There are benches for resting and viewing the scenic lake area. Nonmotorized boating is allowed in the lake, but swimming is not. Visitors will notice neighbors sharing conversation on the trail and hear the laughter and playful calls of local children.

If walking clockwise, you will cross the first boardwalk at 0.4 mile in a cove; a few yards farther is a boat dock. At 0.5 mile is one of the city's signs about trail use and safety regulations. One of the longest boardwalks (238 feet) begins at 0.8 mile, where there are fewer views of residential housing. At the fourth bridge is an attractive marsh. Duck, goose, and other waterfowl are in the low waters between the willow groves. At 1 mile is a **T** junction. To the left, *Lake Lynn Park Trail* ascends, then dips to cross a drainage area and junctions with an unnamed gravel

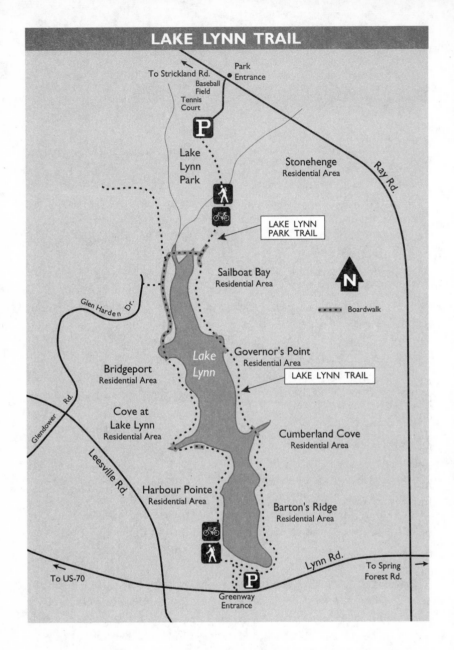

# LAKE LYNN TRAIL

To Strickland Rd.

Park Entrance

Baseball Field

Tennis Court

P

Lake Lynn Park

LAKE LYNN PARK TRAIL

Stonehenge Residential Area

Ray Rd.

Sailboat Bay Residential Area

N

Boardwalk

Glen Harden Dr.

Lake Lynn

Governor's Point Residential Area

LAKE LYNN TRAIL

Bridgeport Residential Area

Glendower Rd.

Cove at Lake Lynn Residential Area

Cumberland Cove Residential Area

Leesville Rd.

Harbour Pointe Residential Area

Barton's Ridge Residential Area

To US-70

Lynn Rd.

To Spring Forest Rd.

P

Greenway Entrance

trail leading to the right to Ray Road. Remain on the asphalt trail. You will ascend to tennis courts and a baseball field at Lake Lynn Park. On the return, you will reach a fifth boardwalk at 1.3 miles and a sixth at 1.6 miles. At 1.8 miles is *Workout Trail*, to the left; it offers physical-fitness stations in a residential housing complex. Cross the grassy dam to return to the point of origin. (USGS maps: Raleigh W and Bayleaf)

## ROCKY MOUNT
### Nash County

The city of Rocky Mount has proposed the development of a Tar River greenway to connect several major parks and recreational facilities such as City Lake, Sunset Park, Battle Park, Tom Stitch Park, and Talbert Park. Call the Parks and Recreation Department for an update.

Battle Park is a 54-acre recreational park, a gift from the Battle family of Rocky Mount Mills. It has a picnic area with shelters, a playground, a boat ramp to the Tar River, and a history trail. After parking, follow *Battle Park Trail* on a paved and easy 1.6-mile loop. You will pass the Donaldson Tavern site, a stagecoach stand from an overland route. Near here, the Marquis de Lafayette was entertained while on his Southern tour in 1825. At 0.2 mile, turn right to the waterfall overlook on the Tar River. Proceed to the playground through a picnic area featuring pine, birch, oak, elm, and dogwood. You will cross the driveway at 1.3 miles and pass the site of the first Rocky Mount post office on the return. This trail is accessible to the physically disabled. An 0.6-mile paved trail has been added. It extends from the loop trail to Church Street. Along the way are two fishing piers and overlooks, a boat launch, and several historic sites, including a turn-of-the-century bridge site, a Tuscarora Indian site, and an old dam site.

*Address and Access:* Parks and Recreation Department, P.O. Drawer 1180, Rocky Mount, NC 27801 (919-972-1151). Access is from the junction of US-64 Bypass and NC-43/48 (Falls Road). Take NC-43/48 southeast 0.5 mile to the parking area near the Confederate monument.

## SMITHFIELD
### Johnston County

*Neuse River Nature Trail* in Town Common Park is maintained by the city's Parks and Recreation Department and the Year-Around Garden

Club. It is an easy 1.6-mile route on the east bank of the Neuse River downtown. From the parking lot on North Front Street, hike 0.2 mile up the east bank to the terminus, then return. Hike downriver past the historic site of Smith's Ferry (1759–86) and under the US-70 bridge at 0.5 mile. Continue through a pristine forest of large sweet gum, oak, and green ash. Turn left at 0.7 mile to reach the tennis courts, the playground, and the parking area on East Market Street (US-70). You will reach South Second Street at 1 mile. Return by the same route or go on North Front Street for a distance of 1.6 miles. Vehicular traffic is allowed on parts of the trail.

*Address and Access:* Director, Parks and Recreation Department, Box 2344, Smithfield, NC 27577 (919-934-9721). Access is on North Front Street one block from East Market Street at the bridge or the East Church Street parking lot.

## WAKE FOREST
### Wake County

H. L. Miller Park has an unnamed 0.3-mile asphalt loop nature trail suitable for wheelchair use. The trail passes among tall loblolly pine, oak, elm, and maple, with an understory of dogwood and mulberry. There are three bridges over a stream, picnic tables, and seats for relaxation. (USGS map: Wake Forest)

*Address and Access:* Parks and Recreation Department, 401 Elm Avenue, Wake Forest, NC 27587 (919-554-6180). From the corner of NC-98 (East Wait Street) and Franklin Street, follow Franklin Street for one block and turn right on East Elm Street. After 0.1 mile, turn right at the recycling site sign. Park to the right of the town hall and enter the forest.

## WILSON
### Wilson County

There are more than 26 parks in Wilson, and many others are proposed. Unnamed walkways are prominent; three areas have designated trails.

The wide *Hominy Canal Trail* is a 0.9-mile path between Ward Boulevard and the junction of Kincaid Avenue and Canal Drive. Tall loblolly pine, willow and live oak, sweet gum, and river birch shade the trail. Access to parking is at Williams Day Camp on Mount Vernon Drive.

The 1.2-mile *Toisnot Lake Trail* circles the lake; it also extends 0.6 mile into the hardwood forest downstream to the Seaboard Coast Railroad. Access to Toisnot Park is on Corbett Avenue to the north near its junction with Ward Boulevard (NC-58/42). Corbett Avenue is also the 3.8-mile access route to Lake Wilson and *Lake Wilson Trail*. Go north 3.3 miles, turn left on Lake Wilson Road (SR-1327) at Dunn's Cross Road, and go 0.5 mile to the lake, on the right.

*Address and Access:* Department of Parks and Recreation, P.O. Box 10, 1800 Herring Avenue (NC-42), Wilson, NC 27894 (919-399-2261). To reach the administrative office, turn west off US-301 onto Herring Avenue (NC-42) and go half a block.

## Lake Wilson Trail

*Length and Difficulty:* 2.3 miles, easy

*Trailhead and Description:* From the parking lot, go either right or left on the dam. If going left, you will cross the dam/spillway and follow an old road through a forest of river birch, alder, sweet gum, and holly. At 0.8 mile, you will bear right off the old road and enter a swampy area; follow the yellow blazes. (Beaver may have dammed the area and prevented crossing.) You will cross a bridge on the feeder stream to an old road at 1.3 miles. Among the swamp vegetation are buttonbush and swamp candle (*Lysimachia terrestris*). Turn right and follow the old road (damaged by four-wheel-drive vehicles) to complete the loop at 2.3 miles. This is a good bird-watching trail.

*Sarah P. Duke Memorial Gardens on the Duke University campus*
*Photo by Clay Nolen, North Carolina Travel and Tourism*

# Chapter 5

# TRAILS ON PRIVATE AND
# UNIVERSITY PROPERTIES

---

Of the 19 million acres of forest in North Carolina, about 13.5 million are owned by private citizens. Named trails on these properties—particularly those trails open to the public—are rare. Some landowners are reluctant to open their properties because of liability and trail abuse. In 1985, there were nearly 200 miles of private trails open to the public; by 1995, there was an 85 percent decrease. The decline continues even though the state legislature passed a bill in 1987 (the Act to Limit the Liability of Landowners to Persons Using Their Land in Connection with the Trails System) to protect private landowners. At least 45 private organizations, resorts, and clubs have trails for their members and associates only.

Regardless of the figures, corporate and individual landowners have a long history of cooperation with Scout troops, schools, nature groups, and hunting and fishing clubs that wish to use their property. Most private trails are not publicized. If all the pathways through farm woodlands, all those favorite fishing and hunting routes, and all those walks to points of meditation were counted, they would number in the thousands. An inquiry to the owners shows respect for their property rights. Frequently, private owners will give an individual or a small group permission to walk a path or roadway if the purpose is for education or aesthetics.

*Primitive crossing of Deep River near the Buckhorn Trail*

# PRIVATE PROPERTY

![BUCKHORN TRAIL heading bar]

## BUCKHORN TRAIL
### Lee County

Until recently, the 45.4-mile, white-blazed *Buckhorn Trail* was the longest hiking trail on private property in the state. It was designed and constructed in the early 1980s by volunteers under the leadership of Frank Barringer of Sanford. Assisting him were Boy Scout Troops 906, 907, 941, 942, and 944 in Lee County and Troop 61 in Lillington. Girl Scout leaders were Jane Barringer and Sylvia Adcock.

From west to east, the trail generally paralleled the Deep River and the Cape Fear River from near the House in the Horseshoe historic site to Raven Rock State Park. The trail meandered through floodplains, steep but low ridges, tributary coves, timberland, and remote areas.

A number of individual landowners participated in the project. Corporate owners included the Federal Paperboard Company, Har-Lee Farm, and Boise-Cascade Corporation. Support and cooperation were given by the hunting clubs of both Lee and Harnett Counties. Campsites were carefully chosen away from developed areas, roads, and streams. No-trace camping was the rule; the same restrictions were in effect that apply to public wilderness areas.

By 1996, the section described below was being maintained by Ralph Meeks, Jr., and Eagle Scout Troop 942. Other sections of the trail have been closed. For information on the progress of reopening them, contact Hal Tysinger, 201 North Steele Street, Sanford, NC 27330 (919-776-2521).

### Section A: Euphronia Church Road to US-421

*Length and Difficulty:* 10.7 miles, moderate

*Trailhead and Description:* From the junction of NC-42 and US-1/15/501 Bypass in Sanford, take NC-42 west for 1.8 miles and turn left on Steel Bridge Road (SR-1318). Go 7.5 miles west to Euphronia Church Road (SR-1393); turn right. It is 0.2 mile to a church parking lot.

Begin the trail on the old forest road leading north past the church cemetery. At 0.5 mile, you will cross the first of a number of small streams. Ahead is a mixed forest of oak, gum, hickory, poplar, pine, holly, hornbeam, wildflowers, and ferns, through which cross many old pioneer wagon roads and more current logging roads. On the right at 1.4 miles are the remains of the McLeod House. (Here also is an alternate, shorter, yellow-blazed trail to the right that rejoins the main trail at 2.3 miles.) At 1.5 miles, you will cross a stream where trout lilies bloom in profusion in March. When the tree leaves are off, the Deep River can be seen from a bluff at 1.9 miles. Remnants of the Blakley House are entwined with yellow jessamine at 2.1 miles. At 2.3 miles, the alternate trail rejoins the main trail near the ruins of another old house.

You will reach a cable gate of the Poe Hunt Club and a massive clear-cut area on the left at 2.8 miles; veer right from the clear-cut on an old woods road. Turn right off the old road onto a footpath at 3.5 miles; this was once the Clark place, now remembered by the escaped jonquils and baby's-breath. At 3.9 miles, you will follow the trail through an area of hardwoods over a rocky streambed, where switch cane and wild grape provide dense understory. You will soon pass left of a young loblolly pine forest. You will cross a tributary of Smith Creek with banks of wildflowers at 4.2 miles and pass under a power line to an old road 0.1 mile later. Turn right off the old road onto a footpath at 4.4 miles in a young forest. Old tobacco rows are evident. At 4.9 miles is an abandoned house on the left 50 yards before NC-42. Turn right to an intersection at 5 miles. (On NC-42, it is 3 miles west to Carbonton and 6.7 miles east to US-1/15/501 in Sanford. To return to Euphronia Church on the roads, go right on Plank Road—SR-1007—and drive 3.7 miles to Steel Bridge Road. Turn right again and drive 2 miles to Euphronia Church Road, on the right.)

Cross the junction diagonally and reenter the forest; you will pass rock piles indicative of pioneer farming. You will cross a stream at 5.6 miles and ascend and descend through former tobacco land now filled with pine, sweet gum, and running cedar. You will then descend to scenic Little Pocket Creek and head downstream (left) at 6 miles. At 6.7 miles, you will cross a small stream on a living holly tree. Ahead, you will cross a number of drains and pass through clear-cuts. You will follow an old logging road and cross Big Pocket Creek on a large, fallen logging bridge at 7.7 miles. Continue on the main road and turn left at a road junction at 8.5 miles. Turn left again on a little-used woods road at 9.1 miles. After 0.1 mile, you will reach the end of the road, where a foot trail begins to the right. (Ahead, 20 yards off the road, is a large, scenic rock ledge with views of the silent and dark Deep River. Hepatica, spring beauty, and trout lily bloom among the ferns in a natural rock garden.) Turn right on the footpath and continue over a high bluff above the river through laurel. You will return to the road at 9.6 miles; a clear-cut may have altered the trail across the road. Turn left and follow the road (formerly Tempting Church Road, SR-1322). You will cross Patterson Creek on an old bridge at 10.5 miles and arrive at US-421 at 10.7 miles.

Gulf is 2 miles to the left. It is 4 miles to the right to US-1/15/501 in Sanford, where a right turn leads 1.8 miles to a junction with NC-42; a right turn on NC-42 and a drive of 4.3 miles returns you to where the trail crossed NC-42. (USGS maps: Goldston, White Hills)

## GREENCROFT GARDENS
### Franklin County

Greencroft Gardens is part of the 83-acre Franklin County Nature Preserve in North Carolina. The preserve and the 178-acre Patrick County Nature Preserve in Virginia are part of De Hart Botanical Gardens, Inc. Founded by Allen and Flora de Hart in 1963, Greencroft Gardens has more than 500 species of plants, trees, shrubs, ferns, and mosses. A prominent species is wild pink (*Silene caroliniana*), a tufted perennial with white, sometimes pink, petals. The property has lakes, streams, springs, rock outcroppings, and wildlife. Open all year without charge or a guide, the preserve is for daytime use only. Space may be reserved for weddings and concerts at the lake amphitheater. Guided tours may be arranged if requested in advance.

*Greencroft Lake Trail* circles the main lake for 0.9 mile. The 0.8-mile *Crane Fly Orchid Trail* begins at the east end of the lake's cross-bridge. There are also the short *Children's Bamboo Trail* near the waterfall and the 275-foot *Trail for the Handicapped* through azaleas from the parking area to the lake. Another 1.1-mile trail is in the planning stage.

Access is from the junction of US-401 and NC-56 West in Louisburg.

*Lake Trail at Greencroft Gardens, part of De Hart Botanical Gardens*

Go south on US-401 for 5.5 miles to the De Hart Botanical Gardens sign. If going north on US-401 from the junction of NC-98, it is 4.4 miles.

*Address:* De Hart Botanical Gardens, Inc., Route 1, Box 36, Louisburg, NC 27549 (919-496-4771 or 919-496-2521)

# LEIGH FARM
Durham County

In 1996, the city and county of Durham and seven other government and private preservation organizations received a second grant from the Natural Heritage Trust Fund—to make a total of $390,000—to preserve the 1834 homeplace of the Richard Stanford Leigh family. New Hope Creek flows through the property. In addition to preserving the historic home and outbuildings in the 86-acre park, plans are to complete a 0.5-mile (currently unnamed) nature trail loop around the home and to create another trail deeper into the forest. Contact the caretaker for updated information.

Access to the park is off I-40, exit 273. Turn east on NC-54, then take the first left (at the dead-end sign). Drive 0.7 mile, partly on a narrow road, to the park. (USGS map: Durham SW)

*Address:* Leigh Farm, 139 Leigh Farm Road, Chapel Hill, NC 27514 (919-496-5002)

# WHITE OAK NATURE TRAIL
Wake County

*White Oak Nature Trail* is an easy 1.5-mile double loop at Carolina Power and Light's Harris Nuclear Power Plant. The skillfully designed and color-coded route begins at a parking and picnic area at the Harris Visitor Center/Energy and Environmental Center. There are interpretive markers about wildlife, trees, ferns, and flowers. The longer part of the loop has boardwalks on the approach to Big Branch, a scenic wetland. Plans are to have talking-tree markers like those at the state forests' educational centers. A trail brochure is available at the trailhead and the visitor center.

To access the trail from US-1 south of Apex, turn off at the New Hill sign to New Hill–Holleman Road (SR-1127) and drive 1.5 miles southeast.

*Address:* Harris Visitor Center, Route 1, Box 327, New Hill, NC 27562 (919-362-3261)

# UNIVERSITY PROPERTIES

Degree programs in parks and recreation are offered at 21 colleges and universities in the state, and 11 two-year colleges offer preliminary degree programs. Some of the large senior institutions offer degrees in forestry and a variety of environmental fields. Two university medical centers—those at the University of North Carolina at Chapel Hill and Duke University—offer departments in recreation therapy. Although few institutions of higher education have adequate property for a trail system, all of them require courses in physical education, and 60 percent have organizations or clubs that promote or sponsor hiking in outings or outdoor sports programs.

## DUKE UNIVERSITY
### Durham, Chatham, Alamance, and Orange Counties

Duke University has two major private areas of natural resources open to the public: the 55-acre Sarah P. Duke Memorial Gardens and the 7,700-acre Duke Forest, composed of six main divisions in four counties. To protect these remarkable properties, the university has provided guidelines and regulations, which are listed in the following descriptions of the Triangle's largest, most varied, and most educationally rewarding network of nature walks.

### Sarah P. Duke Memorial Gardens

The Sarah P. Duke Memorial Gardens have at least 2,000 species of vascular plants. There are three main areas, each emphasizing a variety of local, national, and foreign collections. The Terraces, a memorial gift to Sarah P. Duke by her daughter Frances Biddle Duke, have a wide range of cultivated flowering plants. The Blomquist Garden of Native Plants is a splendid portrayal of 900 species of wildflowers. The Asiatic Arboretum has 550 species of Oriental plants. These special gardens and other sections are blended with manicured allées and paths that grace formal and natural woodland settings. Ponds, lawns, bogs, and forests are part of an artful landscape.

Named in honor of the wife of Benjamin N. Duke, a university founder, the gardens were begun in the early 1930s. They are open daily from 8 A.M. to dusk and are free to the public. For information about reserving space for weddings, special botanical tours, educational programs, or tours for the physically handicapped, call the number below. Garden guidelines are as follows: visitors must not do any damage to the plants, dogs must be on a leash and are not allowed at all in some parts of the gardens, and biking and team sports are not permitted.

*Address and Access:* Sarah P. Duke Memorial Gardens, P.O. Box 90341, Duke University, Durham, NC 27708 (919-484-3698). To access the main entrance, follow Anderson Street between Campus Drive and Erwin Road to a parking area. Parking is not allowed on Flowers Drive (on the northwest border of the gardens).

## Duke Forest

Duke Forest is private property owned and managed by Duke University as an outdoor laboratory for teaching and research. The forest is composed of six main divisions and several smaller tracts. Though access to certain areas is restricted for research purposes, the majority of the forest is open for limited public recreation. Permissible recreational activities are hiking, bicycling (on graded and fire roads only), horseback riding (on graded roads only), picnicking, and fishing. Off-road (single-path) mountain biking is not permitted anywhere in Duke Forest, including the unofficial foot path along New Hope Creek. Group activities must be approved in advance by the forest resource manager.

All roads are gated. Some of them are posted for foot travel only. The regulations for use (also posted at the entrance gates) are as follows: enter only at gated roads; enter at your own risk; walk with a partner; no access is permitted after sunset except at approved picnic sites; do not block gates; unauthorized motor vehicles are prohibited; horses and bicycle traffic must stay on graded and mowed roads; no fires of any kind are allowed; no hunting or shooting of firearms is permitted; no camping is allowed; no vegetation (trees, shrubs, flowers, brush, or grasses) may be cut, picked, scarred, or damaged in any way; dogs

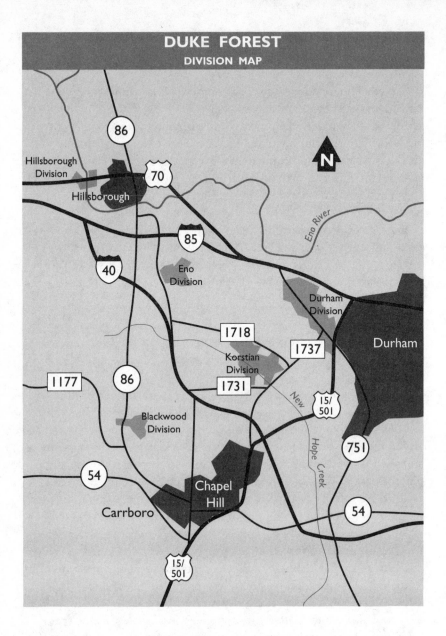

# DUKE FOREST
## DIVISION MAP

86

70

Hillsborough
Division

Hillsborough

85

Eno River

N

40

Eno
Division

Durham
Division

Durham

1718

1737

Korstian
Division

1177

86

1731

15/
501

New

Hope Creek

751

Blackwood
Division

54

Chapel
Hill

Carrboro

54

15/
501

must be kept under control as defined by local ordinance. All visitors must stay on access roads and in designated access areas.

There are three group picnic locations in Duke Forest, all in the Durham Division at gates C, D, and F on NC-751, west of West Campus. These picnic sites have tables and a grill and must be reserved in advance; a fee is charged. There is no running water, and only site F has a pit toilet and electricity. Gates C and F have shelters. The descriptions and maps that follow should provide adequate directional options for the Duke Forest recreational areas. For additional information, contact the Duke Forest Resource Manager, School of the Environment, Room A114, Levine Science Research Center, Box 90332, Durham, NC 27708-0332 (919-613-8013).

## DURHAM DIVISION

The Durham Division has 24 gated roads, nine fire trails, and an interpretive trail. Some are closed for research projects or because entrance is through other private property. Described below are the roads and fire trails currently open. All are accessible on NC-751 with the exception of gated road #14 on Kerley Road, 0.1 mile off NC-751. The gates are numbered 2 through 13; some are on each side of NC-751. It is 2.85 miles west from gate #2 to US-70. If going west on NC-751 from the junction with US-15/501 Bypass, exit 107, drive 0.3 mile and park near gate #2, on the right; this site is 0.7 mile west of the parking area for *Duke Cross Country Trail*, described above.

## Duke Cross Country Trail

*Length and Difficulty:* 2.9 miles (4 miles including physical-fitness and spur trails), easy

*Trailhead and Description:* From US-15/501 Bypass, exit 107, drive east on Cameron Boulevard 0.4 mile to a parking lot on the right at gate #1.

The posted trail guidelines for *Duke Cross Country Trail* indicate that the trail should be used with a partner, that no motorized vehicles are allowed, that hikers must stay off the golf course, and that the trail closes at sunset; the Duke Police Department telephone number is 919-684-2444. The wide gravel trail is almost completely in a wooded area.

If walking counterclockwise, you will pass under a power line at 130 yards, then over the Sandy Creek bridge. Turn left to begin walking parallel to the stream; at the turn is an emergency telephone. You will pass through a grove of river birch and oak with sparkleberry and dogwood as

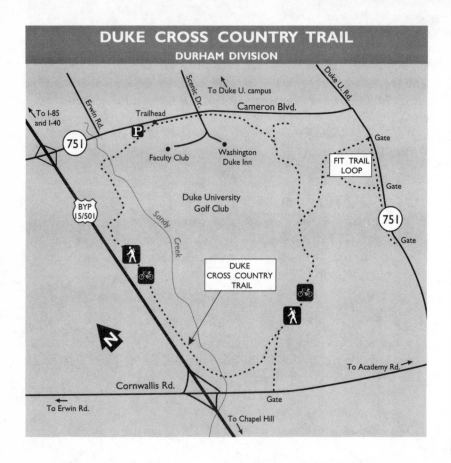

# DUKE CROSS COUNTRY TRAIL
## DURHAM DIVISION

an understory. After a gentle ascent among pines at 0.5 mile, you will note the sound of traffic from US-15/501 Bypass. Another emergency telephone is located at 0.8 mile. To the left are views of the golf course and lakes. At 1.1 miles, you will cross a bridge over Sandy Creek. To the right are a bog and large sycamore trees. You will reach a junction and an emergency telephone at 1.3 miles. (To the right is a 0.1-mile paved spur trail that exits to Cornwallis Road and roadside parking.)

You will then ascend to views of the golf course, pass an emergency telephone at 1.8 miles, and enter a forest of oak, poplar, and sycamore. The understory has black cohosh, mandrake, and buckeye. There is a junction at 2 miles with a paved spur leading to the right to *Fitness Trail*. (If using *Fitness Trail*, walk 0.1 mile to where it begins. The trail has 32 stations in its loop and passes through a loblolly pine forest for 0.6 mile.

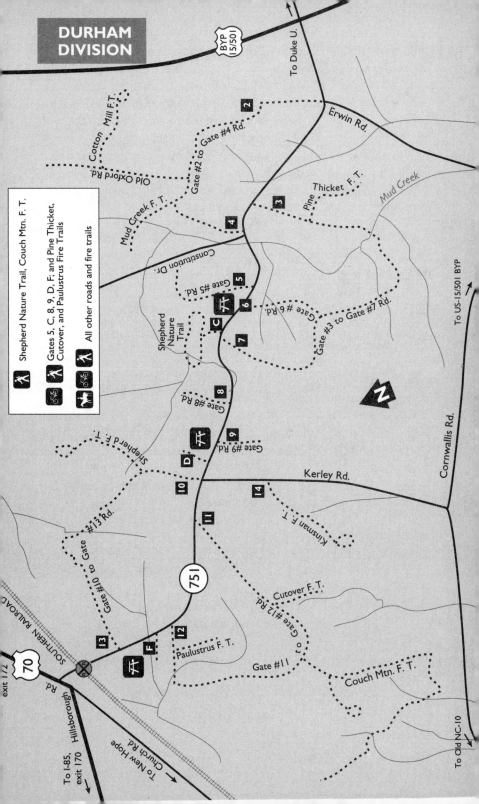

It offers parking from Cameron Boulevard and an emergency telephone.) Continuing on *Duke Cross Country Trail*, you will cross a wooden bridge in a forest of large white oak. At 2.3 miles are another emergency telephone, a water fountain, and a junction with a paved spur leading right. (The spur goes 130 yards to a locked gate at a soccer field.) You will pass the open gates to a large parking field, to the right. At 2.5 miles, you will cross the entrance road to the Washington Duke Inn and Golf Club, on the left. You will also cross an entrance road to the Duke Faculty Club, on the left. Back on the trail, you will begin a slight descent through the forest and complete the trail at 2.9 miles.

**Gate #2 to Gate #4 Road** *(1 mile, easy)*
**Old Oxford Road** *(0.6 mile round-trip, easy)*
**Cotton Mill Fire Trail** *(0.6 mile round-trip, easy)*
**Mud Creek Fire Trail** *(0.4 mile round-trip, easy)*

Enter the gate and walk under a power line. After 0.1 mile, you will follow a foot trail straight through woods to avoid the front lawn of a residence. You will return to the road at 0.4 mile and enter a longleaf pine forest planted in 1933 and thinned in 1988.

If including fire trails on your walk, turn right at 0.6 mile on historic *Old Oxford Road*, with its compact cobblestones; a young forest to the left allows sunlight. After 295 yards, you will junction with *Cotton Mill Fire Trail*, on the right, a beautiful path on a grassy road under large oak, shagbark hickory, and red cedar; flowers are scattered along the trail. You will reach a cul-de-sac and note the sound of traffic from US-15/501 Bypass at 1.1 miles. You will then return to *Old Oxford Road*. Turn right. At 1.5 miles, you will reach a dead end at an apartment complex. Retrack to Gate #2 to Gate #4 Road and turn right on a gravel road at 1.8 miles. You will pass through a forest where a timber harvest has been made of loblolly pine planted in 1932. Make a right turn at 2 miles to follow *Mud Creek Fire Trail*. It descends through a rocky area to cross a small stream in a forest of oak, poplar, and hickory. At 2.2 miles, you will reach the end of the trail near a housing development. Return to Gate #2 to Gate #4 Road, turn right, and follow the road through tall loblolly pine to gate #4 at NC-751 at 2.6 miles.

On the highway, it is 0.6 mile east to gate #2, for a round-trip distance of 3.2 miles. (USGS map: Durham NW)

## Gate #3 Road to Gate #7 Road *(2.6 miles round-trip, easy)*

Park on the roadside at Gate #3 Road, located 0.3 mile west of gate #2. You will enter a combined hardwood and pine forest and arrive at *Pine Thicket Fire Trail* at 0.1 mile. Turn left. You will reach a boundary sign after 0.3 mile. Return to Gate #3 Road and turn left at 0.7 mile. You will cross a wooden bridge over Mud Creek at 0.9 mile. Here are tall poplar, oak, and loblolly pine; on the forest floor are wild ginger, fire pink, New Jersey tea, wild quinine, and coreopsis. You will then ascend gradually through tall trees and pass a seed forest of 1926. Over the years, the area has been thinned six times; some prescribed burns for timber harvesting were made in the 1980s. You will descend slightly and cross a small tributary of Mud Creek at 1.3 miles. At 1.5 miles, you will junction with Gate #6 Road, on the right. (Gate #6 Road descends on a duff-covered road and through a shady forest with buckeye in damp areas; it reaches NC-571 after 0.3 mile. It is 0.4 mile on NC-571 to Gate #3 Road, for a total loop of 2.2 miles.) At 1.6 miles on Gate #3 Road to Gate #7 Road, you will pass a forest salvage cut made in 1987 because of pine beetle infestation. You will reach Gate #7 Road at NC-751 at 2.1 miles.

It is 0.5 mile east on NC-571 to Gate #3 Road, for a total of 2.6 miles. (USGS map: Durham NW)

## Gate C Road and Shepherd Nature Trail *(1 mile, easy)*

Gate C Road is across NC-571 a few yards east of Gate #7 Road. After entering the gate, go 250 yards to *Shepherd Nature Trail*, on the left, a 0.8-mile interpretive loop trail around the Gate C Road picnic area. (Ahead on the road, it is 350 feet to the Bobby Ross Jr. Memorial Shelter, which has tables and a grill but no water or restrooms.) If hiking the nature trail, enter at the sign that credits the trail to Eagle Scout Troop 440, Duke Forest, and the National Civilian Community Corps. You will descend on switchbacks and cross a footbridge over a tributary of Mud Creek. You will then ascend and pass a number of interpretive markers at such trees as Eastern red cedar, white oak, sweet gum, and pine. At 0.5 mile, you will cross the stream again on a footbridge; to the right is an old farm spring. You will then ascend to Gate #5 Road. (To the left, the road goes 240 yards to end at a housing development. To the right is a forest path to the picnic shelter.) *Shepherd Nature Trail* goes ahead on

Gate #5 Road for 280 feet before turning right off the road. (Gate #5 Road goes 0.2 mile to NC-751.) Continuing on the nature trail, exit at the south side of the picnic shelter at 0.7 mile. Turn left on the gravel road to reach the point of origin at 0.8 mile and make your way back to NC-751 at 1 mile. (USGS map: Durham NW)

## Gate #9 Road *(0.4 mile round-trip, easy)*

This is a solitary, infrequently used, level, 960-foot path through a mixed young forest to the forest property line; backtrack. From here, it is 0.2 mile west to Kerley Road (SR-1309) and 0.05 mile east to Gate #8 Road.

## Gate #14, Kinsman Fire Trail *(0.4 mile round-trip, easy)*

From the junction of Kerley Road and NC-751, go south 0.1 mile to gate #14, on the right, to enter *Kinsman Fire Trail*. This is a pleasant, grassy trail among oak and pine with an understory of sourwood and dogwood dappled with sunlight. Two large oak trees form a center-piece at the cul-de-sac at 0.2 mile. Backtrack.

## Gate D Road and Picnic Area *(0.2 mile round-trip, easy)*

Gate D is on the north side of NC-751; it is located 290 feet east of gate #10 at the junction of Kerley Road. This gravel road leads 0.1 mile to a picnic table and grill under a large, spreading white oak. The impressive tree is typical of many locations in Duke Forest, where white oak predominates. Backtrack.

## Gate #10 Road to Gate #13 Road *(1.9 miles, easy)*

Using a second vehicle at either end of this hike is an advantage.

If beginning at Gate #10 Road, you will follow a gravel road used frequently by staff to reach Global Climate Research, a restricted research site off the south side of the road. At 0.1 mile, turn right on *Shepherd Fire Trail*, a route covered in duff and grass. After another 0.1 mile, turn onto an unnamed fire trail that leads 0.2 mile in and back; the scenic road boasts huge oak and hickory. Continuing on *Shepherd Fire Trail*, you will pass under a large power line to reach a cul-de-sac at 0.7 mile; wildflowers such as stone clover, yarrow, goldenrod, sneezeweed, and aster grow under the power line. Along the road banks are dogwood, deciduous holly, and downy arrowwood (*Viburnum rafinesquianum*).

Return to Gate #10 Road to Gate #13 Road and turn right. On the right is a loblolly pine plantation planted in 1933 and thinned in 1954 and 1988, an example of the skillful silviculture throughout Duke Forest. On the left is another pine grove, planted in 1971 and thinned in 1991. You will arrive at a power line at 1 mile, then pass a restricted gravel road, to the left. Wildflowers are along the road and under the power line. You will cross a small stream and pass the main entrance to Global Climate Research. You will then curve left at 1.4 miles to parallel a Southern Railroad line for the next 0.3 mile; the grassy road is bordered with willow in a wide forest space. Turn left at 1.8 miles. You will arrive at Gate #13 Road on NC-751 at 1.9 miles. Backtrack or follow the highway to the left for 0.8 mile to return to Gate #10 Road. To the right on NC-751 and across the railroad bridge, it is 0.3 mile to the junction with US-70. (USGS maps: Durham NW, Hillsborough)


## Gate #11 Road to Gate #12 Road, Couch Mountain Fire Trail
*(3.2 miles or 5.4 miles round-trip, moderate)*

Making these roads and fire trails into a loop and backtracking offers the longest hiking experience in the Durham Division. A main feature is the ascent of Couch Mountain, 640 feet in elevation.

Enter Gate #11 Road; you will pass a timber restoration of 1993 and 1996, to the left. At 0.1 mile, you will pass an unnamed restricted road, to the left; on the right is a forest management demonstration area. At 0.3 mile, you will cross a small stream in a mixed forest of hardwoods and pine. You will junction with *Cutover Fire Trail* at 0.45 mile; turn left. (Regardless of the fire trail's name, this is a thriving and maturing hardwood and loblolly pine forest.) After crossing a level area, you will descend to the forest property line. Backtrack to Gate #11 Road at 0.9 mile and turn left. You will then follow an undulation through an all-pine forest and reach a major triangle junction at 1.4 miles. To the right is part of the return loop; to the left is an ascent of Couch Mountain.

If hiking left, you will ascend 325 feet to *Couch Mountain Fire Trail*, left and ahead. Ascend ahead; you will reach the summit at 1.6 miles and circle the cul-de-sac in a high forest of oak, hickory, and pine enlivened by a showy display of dogwood in springtime. You will return to *Couch Mountain Fire Trail* at 1.8 miles. The choices here are to turn right and include an additional 2.1 miles in your hike or to descend to the triangle and complete the loop. (*Couch Mountain Fire Trail* soon begins a 1-mile descent before reaching a ridge climb near the trail's end. At a few steep sections, there is road erosion. The sound of traffic from I-85 can be heard. Along the way are downy arrowwood and dogwood among a mixed forest. At 0.2 mile are large shagbark hickory. At 0.6 mile in a hollow are crested dwarf iris. At 0.7 mile, the forest hillside has a spectacular grove of large white oak. After two switchbacks, you will descend into an open area among blackberry bushes; you will reach gate #20 at private property. Backtrack for a round-trip of 2.1 miles.)

Continuing on the loop, you will descend to the triangle junction. Turn left at 1.85 miles (4 miles if including *Couch Mountain Fire Trail*). You will gradually descend on a well-graded road among hardwoods to a junction with a power line at 2.2 miles in an open area. Turn right (east) to junction with *Paulustrus Fire Trail*, located on the right at 2.3 miles. Follow it to a dead end for a 0.4-mile round-trip through a pine forest with a ground cover of club moss. Exit at Gate #12 Road to NC-751 at 2.7 miles (4.8 miles if including *Couch Mountain Fire Trail*).

To the right on NC-751, it is 0.5 mile to Gate #11 Road, for a total distance of 3.2 miles (5.3 miles if including *Couch Mountain Fire Trail*). To the left (west) on NC-751, it is 0.1 mile to the entrance to picnic area F and 280 yards on the entrance road to the R. L. Rigsbee Picnic Shelter, which offers tables, a grill, a pit toilet, and electricity; reservations and a fee are necessary for usage. Farther northwest on NC-751, it is 0.1 mile to gate #13, on the right, described above. It is another 0.3 mile to US-70 (Hillsborough Road). A left turn on US-70 leads 1.5 miles to I-85, exit 170; a right turn leads 1.2 miles to another junction with I-85 (probably exit 172 when 1996 construction is completed). Another 1.3 miles east is a junction with US-15/501 Bypass. (USGS maps: Durham NW, Hillsborough)

## KORSTIAN DIVISION

The 1,950-acre Korstian Division of Duke Forest is located southwest of the Durham Division between Mount Sinai Road (SR-1718) on the north and Whitfield Road (SR-1731) on the south. A distinctive feature is New Hope Creek, which originates in the hills west of the division and flows through the forest, then between Durham and Chapel Hill south into Jordan Lake. Snaking through the New Hope Creek gorge, the stream is usually silted with its upstream soils. Seventeen gated roads and fire trails are in the division. Concrete Bridge Road (gates #25 and #23) and Wooden Bridge Road (gate #24) are frequently used by walkers, joggers, runners, bikers, equestrians, and families with children and pets. Visitors must not go beyond the turnarounds at the ends of roads; trailblazing and footpath shortcuts to New Hope Creek are fobidden and result in severe erosion.

Using the two main gated forest roads, both of which cross New Hope Creek, visitors can enjoy an 11-mile loop hike, the longest option in the forest divisions; a second vehicle may be used for convenience by those hiking only half the distance.

Access is from US-15/501 Bypass, exit 107; drive west 0.3 mile on Cameron Boulevard, then turn left on Erwin Road at the Duke Forest sign. Follow Erwin Road for 3.1 miles (you will pass a junction with Mount Sinai Road at 1.75 miles) and turn right on Whitfield Road. Drive 0.85 mile to Gate #25 Concrete Bridge Road, on the right. To access the other end of the loop, drive 0.5 mile farther on Whitfield Road to a narrow entrance on the right and Gate #24 Wooden Bridge Road. (From that point on Whitfield Road, it is 2.05 miles to a junction with NC-86 and I-40, exit 266. The northern access of Concrete Bridge Road is 2.05 miles west on Mount Sinai Road from Erwin Road, or 3 miles east on Mount Sinai Road from NC-86.)

## Gate #25 Concrete Bridge Road and Gate #24 Wooden Bridge Road (10.3 miles, moderate)
**Concrete Bridge Road** (1.8 miles, easy)
**Hard Climb Road** (1.2 miles round-trip, moderate)
**Midway Fire Trail** (0.6 mile round-trip, easy)
**Thrift Fire Trail** (0.4 mile round-trip, easy)
**Echinata Fire Trail** (0.5 mile round-trip, easy)
**Big Bend Fire Trail** (0.2 mile round-trip, easy)
**Wooden Bridge Road** (1.9 miles, easy to moderate)
**Dead End Fire Trail** (0.4 mile round-trip, easy)
**Land's End Fire Trail** (0.4 mile round-trip, easy)

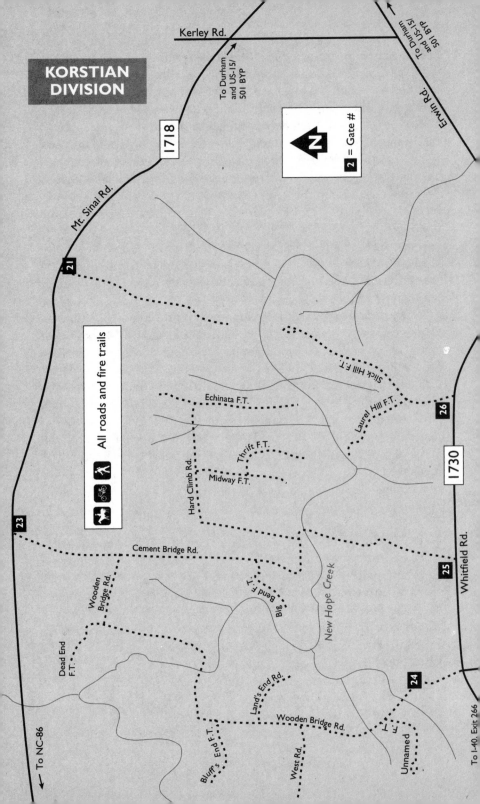

**KORSTIAN DIVISION**

Kerley Rd.

To Durham and US-15/ 501 BYP

To Durham and US-15/ 501 BYP

Erwin Rd.

N

**2** = Gate #

1718

Mt. Sinai Rd.

**21**

All roads and fire trails

Slick Hill F.T.

Echinata F.T.

Laurel Hill F.T.

**26**

Thrift F.T.

Hard Climb Rd.

Midway F.T.

1730

Whitfield Rd.

**23**

Cement Bridge Rd.

**25**

Wooden Bridge Rd.

New Hope Creek

Big Bend F.T.

Dead End F.T.

Land's End Rd.

**24**

Bluff's End F.T.

West Rd.

Wooden Bridge Rd.

Unnamed F.T.

To NC-86

To I-40, Exit 266

## Bluff's End Fire Trail *(0.5 mile round-trip, easy)*
## West Road *(0.6 mile round-trip, easy)*
## Unnamed fire trail *(0.4 mile round-trip, easy)*

Enter Gate #25 Concrete Bridge Road, a gravel road, among tall hardwoods and pine. You will gradually descend to cross New Hope Creek on a low-water cement bridge at 0.6 mile. After 315 feet, you will junction with Hard Climb Road, to the right. Ascend steeply; at 1.1 miles, you will junction with *Midway Fire Trail*, on the right. Turn right on a grassy route to descend to a junction with *Thrift Fire Trail*, on the left. Continue on *Midway Fire Trail* to a cemetery on the right at 1.3 miles. You will reach the rim of the New Hope Creek gorge at 1.4 miles. Backtrack to *Thrift Fire Trail* at 1.6 miles. Turn right and follow it to a timber harvest at 1.8 miles, where patches of wild quinine and aster flourish in a sunny area. Return to Midway Fire Road, turn right, and return to Hard Climb Road at 2.15 miles. Turn right. You will cross a small drain and junction with *Echinata Fire Trail*, on the right at 2.3 miles. Turn right. You will enter a timber cut prompted by a pine beetle infestation, then descend to a cul-de-sac near the rim of the New Hope Creek gorge. After a return to the junction with Hard Climb Road at 2.8 miles, turn left. (The road to the north is not maintained and goes to private property.) Backtrack to Concrete Bridge Road at 3.4 miles.

Turn right on Concrete Bridge Road. At 3.5 miles, you will pass a timber cut prompted by a pine beetle infestation in 1994. At 3.7 miles, you will reach the top of the hill. Turn left on *Big Bend Fire Trail*, which ends at the rim of a bend in New Hope Creek at 3.8 miles. Backtrack to Concrete Bridge Road and turn left. At 4.1 miles, a development of private homes is noticeable through the forest to the right. You will follow a generally straight road to a junction with Wooden Bridge Road at 4.5 miles. The options here are to turn left and make a loop back to Whitfield Road at 8.2 miles or to continue to gate #23 on Mount Sinai Road at 4.8 miles.

If continuing to gate #23, you will find roadside space for parking, but do not block gates. On Mount Sinai Road, it is 1.9 miles east to Kerley Road and 3 miles west to NC-86. If backtracking, turn right at Wooden Bridge Road; you will pass through a large area of reforestation and reach a **T** junction at 5.3 miles. A right turn leads 200 feet to *Dead End Fire Trail*, on the left. (Straight ahead, it is 0.2 mile to the forest property line; backtrack.) On *Dead End Fire Trail*, you will cross a small stream and reach a cul-de-sac at 6 miles. Backtrack to Wooden Bridge Road and turn right at 5.8 miles. It is 0.4 mile through tall oak, maple, and pine to the New Hope Creek wooden bridge; the creek has a rocky streambed and occasional pools under overhanging hardwood trees. You will ascend steeply to cross under a Duke Power Company power line at 6.4 miles, then turn right on *Bluff's End Fire Trail* at 6.5 miles. Located on a tranquil and little-traveled ridge line above the creek, the trail dead-ends and makes a return after 0.5 mile. You will pass under the power line again and arrive at Land's End Road, located on the left at 7.1 miles. Follow it east, first on a level ridge, then descending southeast toward the rim of the gorge at 7.5 miles. Backtrack and turn left on Wooden Bridge Road.

At 8 miles, turn right on West Road. You will pass under the power line again and reenter the forest at 8.2 miles. Here are red mulberry, black cohosh, buckeye, and redbud. The road ends at the forest property line at 8.3 miles. Backtrack to Wooden Bridge Road and turn right to begin a long descent. You will cross an intermittent tributary of New Hope Creek at 8.9 miles. After 225 feet, turn right on an unnamed fire trail; it has a cul-de-sac and leads 0.4 mile round-trip. You will continue through a majestic part of the forest, cross a small stream, ascend, and reach a narrow roadside parking area 200 feet beyond gate #24 at 9.7 miles. It is 0.1 mile on a narrow entrance road to Whitfield Road and 0.5 mile east on the road to roadside parking at Gate #25 Concrete Bridge Road, for a total loop of 10.3 miles.

To the west on Whitfield Road, it is 2.1 miles to NC-86 and I-40, exit 266. (USGS map: Hillsborough)

## Gate #26 Laurel Hill Fire Trail, Slick Hill Fire Trail
*(1 mile round-trip, moderate)*

It is 0.3 mile east on Whitfield Road from Gate #25 Concrete Bridge Road to *Laurel Hill Fire Trail*.

You will ascend slightly for 0.2 mile to junction with *Slick Hill Fire Trail*, on the right. Continue left on *Laurel Hill Fire Trail*, descending to a cul-de-sac and cliffs at 0.4 mile. To the right are switchbacks into the New Hope Creek gorge; they lead among rocks to the creek side at 0.5 mile. Backtrack to *Slick Hill Fire Trail* at 0.8 mile and turn left. You will descend and level off on a ridge, then descend again through a hardwood forest with an understory of huckleberry, downy arrowwood, and dogwood. You will reach a cul-de-sac at 1.4 miles. Backtrack to Whitfield Road at 2.2 miles. (USGS map: Chapel Hill)

*Slick Hill Fire Trail in Korstian Division of Duke Forest*

## Gate #21 Piney Mountain Fire Trail *(1 mile round-trip, easy)*

*Piney Mountain Fire Trail* is on the north side of the Korstian Division at gate #21, across the road from Mount Sinai Baptist Church on Mount Sinai Road. If traveling from US-15/501 Bypass, exit 107, go 0.3 mile west on Cameron Boulevard and turn left on Erwin Road at the Duke Forest sign.

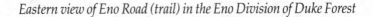

*Eastern view of Eno Road (trail) in the Eno Division of Duke Forest*

Follow Erwin Road 1.9 miles to a junction on the right with Mount Sinai Road, then drive 1 mile farther to roadside parking on the left.

This pleasant, grassy fire trail has pine, maple, and oak with an understory of redbud, dogwood, downy arrowwood, and sourwood. After 0.3 mile, you will reach a new white-pine plantation, planted in 1975. Wildlife tracks may be visible in some of the shallow roadside ditches. At 0.5 mile is a high, breezy rim above New Hope Creek. A picnic table is here among tall oak trees. Backtrack. (USGS map: Chapel Hill)


## ENO DIVISION

The 519-acre Eno Division is southeast of Hillsborough and west of Eno River State Park, between I-85 and I-40. Stony Creek runs through the division on its way east to the Eno River in Eno River State Park. The main artery in the division is Eno Road from gate #28 to NC-86. Although *Flat Rock Fire Trail* is scenic and *Oak Hill Fire Trail* is historic, this division does not have many users. All of its pathways are described below.


## Gate #28 Eno Road

*Access:* If driving west in Durham on I-85, turn off at exit 172 onto US-70. After 1.3 miles, turn left immediately past the traffic lights onto Old NC-10 (SR-1710). Drive 3.75 miles to the junction with New Hope Church Road (SR-1723); turn left. After 0.4 mile, you will reach gate #28, on the right.

If driving from I-40, take exit 263 and follow New Hope Church Road 2.1 miles to gate #28, on the left; on the way, you will cross NC-86 at 0.7 mile.

If approaching from I-85, exit 165, drive south on NC-86 for 0.4 mile to Old NC-10, on the left; look closely after the I-85 exit because the road is easy to miss. Drive 2.1 miles to the junction with New Hope Church Road and turn right. Drive 0.4 mile to the roadside parking on the right.

From the junction of NC-86 and New Hope Church Road, it is 1.2 miles north on NC-86 to the Hillsborough District of the North Carolina Forest Service (right) and gate #29. This trailhead can also be reached from I-85, exit 165, by following NC-86 south for 1.6 miles. Because the forest service gate is locked each day at 5 P.M., park outside the forest gate.

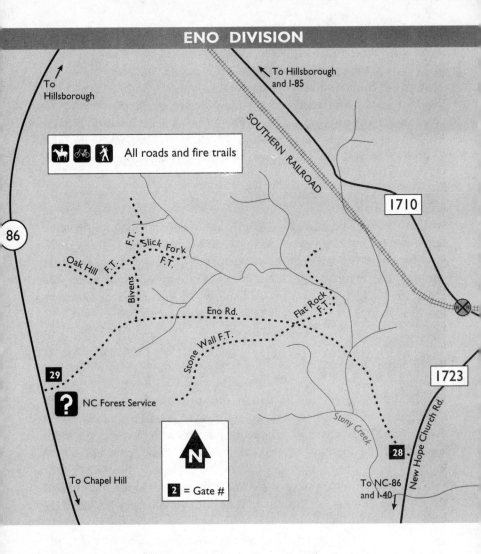

🐎 🚲 🚶 All roads and fire trails

86

1710

Oak Hill F.T.

Slick Fork F.T.

Bivens F.T.

Eno Rd.

Flat Rock F.T.

Stone Wall F.T.

29

? NC Forest Service

N

**2** = Gate #

To Hillsborough

To Hillsborough and I-85

SOUTHERN RAILROAD

1723

New Hope Church Rd.

Stony Creek

28

To Chapel Hill

To NC-86 and I-40

**Gate #28 Eno Road** *(1.4 miles, easy)*
**Flat Rock Fire Trail** *(0.7 mile round-trip, easy)*
**Stone Wall Fire Trail** *(1.3 miles round-trip, easy)*
**Bivens Fire Trail** *(0.8 mile round-trip, easy)*
**Oak Hill Fire Trail** *(0.7 mile round-trip, easy)*
**Slick Rock Fire Trail** *(0.4 mile round-trip, easy)*

From gate #28 on Eno Road, you will enter a forest of tall trees, then a new forest at 0.4 mile. You will cross Stony Creek in an area of tall poplar and low patches of filbert and buckeye, then enter an open area; to the left is evidence of a timber harvest. You will gradually ascend to a junction with *Flat Rock Fire Trail*, to the right at 0.6 mile. Follow *Flat Rock Fire Trail*. At 0.7 mile, you will cross a footbridge over gurgling, rocky Stony Creek. Here are mosses, pinxter, and rattlesnake orchid. You will reach the end of the road at 0.8 mile; backtrack. Turn right at Eno Road. Within 50 feet, turn left on *Stone Wall Fire Trail*, where you will see evidence of timber harvesting, thinning, and a planting process. Colic root grows on the roadside. You will reach a tributary of Stony Creek at 1.9 miles. Backtrack to Eno Road and turn left at 2.5 miles. The road passes through a young forest and descends to enter an older forest. You will cross an intermittent stream at 2.9 miles. You will then ascend, pass a timber management area, located to the left, and arrive at *Bivens Fire Trail* at 3.1 miles.

Turn right. You will pass through a forest of hardwoods and pine to a junction with *Oak Hill Fire Trail* at 3.3 miles. Turn left and ascend in a pine forest to the rock foundation of a farm building, on the left at 3.4 miles, then cross an imposing level area to a hilltop of oak trees at 3.6 miles. Backtrack to *Bivens Fire Trail* and turn left. After 110 feet, turn right on *Slick Rock Fire Trail*. You will descend slightly on a rarely used road to a small stream for a respite among spicebush, jack-in-the-pulpit, and green and gold. Backtrack to *Bivens Fire Trail* at 4.3 miles. Turn right, descend, and enter a section where timber was harvested in 1996. After crossing a small stream, you will ascend to the forest boundary at 4.5 miles. Backtrack to Eno Road at 5 miles. A right turn leads 0.2 mile to gate #29 at the maintenance area of the North Carolina Forest Service, for a total hike of 5.3 miles. Or you can backtrack another 1 mile on Eno Road to gate #28 for a total of 6.3 miles. (USGS map: Hillsborough)

## HILLSBOROUGH DIVISION

In this 645-acre division are old and currently used quarries of blue stone. The division has also been used in timber harvesting, particularly of shortleaf and loblolly pine. Two of the forest roads have trailheads close to each other on US-70. The other road is farther west and off US-70. All are on the west side of Hillsborough. The Eno River flows north to south through the division, and US-70 runs east-west. Only one fire road is open to the public for hiking. Hikers may notice many young

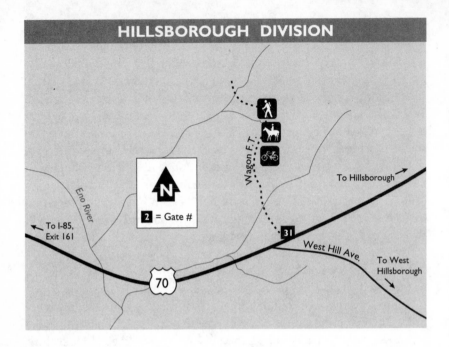

To Hillsborough

To I-85,
Exit 161

To West
Hillsborough

West Hill Ave.

Eno River

Wagon F.T.

2 = Gate #

70

pines in the Hillsborough Division. This is because of damage to older forests in the November, 1992 tornado.

### Gate #31 Wagon Fire Trail (1.2 miles round-trip, easy)

Access to Gate #31 *Wagon Fire Trail* is on the north side of US-70 (Cornelius Street) 1.5 miles west of the junction with NC-86 (Churston Street) in Hillsborough. From the west, take exit 161 off I-85 and go 0.9 mile to US-70, then 1 mile east on US-70 to the gate, located on the left near the junction with West Hill Avenue.

Enter the gate. You will cross a small stream at 0.3 mile in an area damaged by a tornado in 1992. A stand of pine was replanted in 1994. Skullcap, coreopsis, aster, wild indigo, buttercup, and wild rose grow on the road banks. Deer may be seen in the grassy areas. At 0.3 mile, you will enter a forest of tall pine; periwinkle is on the north side of the road. You will cross a small stream and reach the trail's end at 0.6 mile. Backtrack for a round-trip hike of 1.2 miles. (USGS map: Efland)

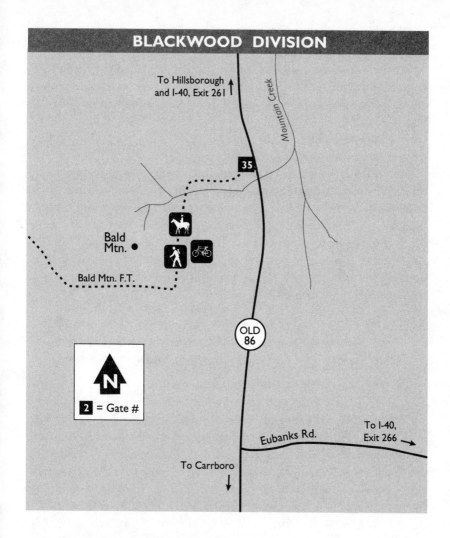

# BLACKWOOD DIVISION

The Blackwood Division offers unique topography, the forest's highest hill (Bald Mountain, 762 feet in elevation), and part of a swamp known as Meadow Flats. The division is comprised of one large tract and three smaller tracts. In the division's 998 acres are 16 compartments and 11 roads and fire trails. Because of restricted research, the routes to seven of these roads and trails are closed north of Eubanks Road (SR-1727). Two other short fire trails have private access in a separate tract near Blackwood Mountain, but the enchanting 1.1-mile fire trail described below is open to the public on the west side of Old NC-86.

**Bald Mountain Fire Trail** (*2.2 miles round-trip, easy*)

Access to the fire trail is 4.1 miles south on Old NC-86 (SR-1009) from its junction with I-85, exit 261. There is also an access from I-40, exit 266. Drive west for 3.2 miles on Eubanks Road (SR-1717) to Old NC-86. After a right turn, it is 0.8 mile to the fire trail, on the left (west). Parking is limited, and neighbors discourage parking on their driveway.

You will enter the forest on a grassy road and ascend slightly at 0.3 mile. At 0.5 mile are a poplar about 14 feet in circumference and a large patch of crested dwarf iris. You will curve around the south slope of Bald Mountain in an oak/hickory forest and follow the edge of the forest boundary markers. Deer, squirrel, raccoon, and owl inhabit the area. At 0.9 mile, you will cross a ridge in a pristine setting. You will then descend to the trail's end between pine and hickory at 1.1 miles. Backtrack. (USGS map: Chapel Hill)

# NORTH CAROLINA STATE UNIVERSITY
### Wake, Durham, and Moore Counties

Carl A. Schenck Memorial Forest is a research laboratory of conifers and broadleaves on the university property between Wade Avenue and Reedy Creek Park Road (SR-1650) in Raleigh. The 6-mile *Loblolly Trail* (see the Richland Creek Area section of the coverage of Raleigh in chapter 4) goes 1.5 miles through the forest, and the 1.2-mile *Frances Liles Interpretive Trail* is in the forest interior. The latter trail has 10 stops that describe the multiple benefits derived from forestland. Redbud groves and pine grafting are prominent on the south side of the loop. Access is either from *Loblolly Trail* or the picnic shelter. To reach the picnic shelter, take Reedy Creek Park Road off Blue Ridge Road 1 mile north of the state fairgrounds and go 0.9 mile to the forest entrance sign, on the left. Go 0.1 mile to the entrance gate and park to avoid blocking the gate. Walk on the gated road 0.1 mile to the picnic shelter (right) and the trailhead. (USGS map: Raleigh W)

The 2,400-acre Hill Forest is in Durham County north of Durham and southeast of Rougemont. It has a network of forest roads that may be used by the public for day-hiking. Permission is required; if you cannot reach the caretaker at 919-477-1125, call the NCSU number listed below. Camping and hunting are not allowed. The forest is on both sides of the Flat River, which flows into Lake Michie and then Falls Lake; State Forest Road (SR-1614) provides an access bridge to either side.

To reach the forest from I-85 in Durham, drive 12.5 miles north on US-501 to the Quail Roost community and turn right on Moores Mill Road (SR-1601); from Rougemont, go 2 miles south on US-501 and turn left on Moores Mill Road. Turn right immediately on the gravel State Forest Road. The entrance to George K. Slocum Forestry Camp and the caretaker's office is on the left after 0.8 mile. Reserved camping is allowed beyond the office.

Because the forest roads are not named or numbered, the following descriptions are designated as the first, second, third, and fourth nature walks.

For the first nature walk, continue east on State Forest Road for 0.3 mile from the access to Slocum Forestry Camp, descending to a left curve. On the right of the curve is the forest road entrance; parking in this area is difficult. You will ascend on a narrow road and pass through a pine forest planted in 1952 and thinned in 1982; a prescribed burn was done here in 1992. Along the roadside are sensitive pea, selfheal, and wild basil. On the right at 0.2 mile is a young forest of poplar planted in 1978. You will cross a rocky stream at 0.4 mile and ascend in an older forest of large white oak. Parts of the roadway are eroded. The road then levels off. At 0.8 mile, you will enter a pine forest planted in 1962. You will descend, pass an old, eroded road (left), and enter a mature loblolly pine forest at 1.4 miles. You will pass an area of harvested timber and exit at Quail Roost Road (SR-1615) at 1.6 miles. To the right, it is 1.2 miles to US-501; another right turn leads 0.4 mile to Moores Mill Road, on the right.

The second nature walk begins across the Flat River 0.2 mile from the beginning of the walk described above. Cross the bridge on State Forest Road and ascend steeply in a curve to a forest road on the right. Again, there is only roadside parking. Walk past the gate, which may be open during the summer months. You will pass through a loblolly pine plantation, then enter an open space before entering a forest of Virginia yellow pine at 0.2 mile; you will notice a sign forbidding road usage by equestrians and bikers. You will then descend to a low area among oak, maple, poplar, and holly. You will ascend to a stand of pine on the right and pass an old tobacco barn and other abandoned buildings before

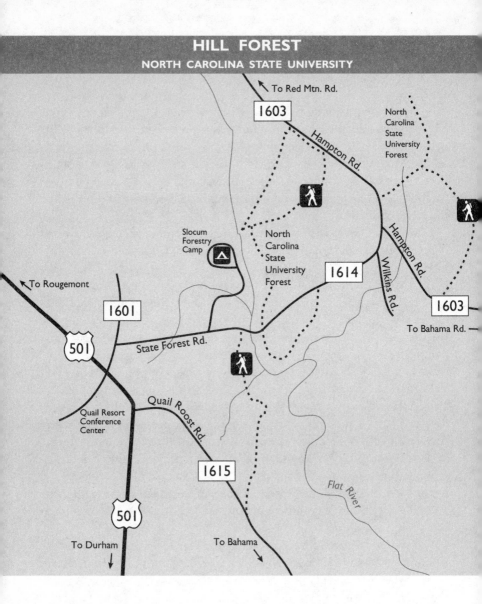

## HILL FOREST
### NORTH CAROLINA STATE UNIVERSITY

To Red Mtn. Rd.

1603

Hampton Rd.

North Carolina State University Forest

Slocum Forestry Camp

North Carolina State University Forest

1614

Wilkins Rd.

Hampton Rd.

1603

To Bahama Rd.

To Rougemont

1601

501

State Forest Rd.

Quail Resort Conference Center

Quail Roost Rd.

1615

Flat River

501

To Durham

To Bahama

exiting to State Forest Road at 1.2 miles. To the left, it is 0.5 mile on the gravel road to where you started.

The third trail, which may also be hiked as a loop, has an entrance across State Forest Road from where you began the second trail. You will enter a narrow but more frequently used road and pass through a young forest for 0.4 mile. At 0.75 mile is a magnificent stand of white pine planted in 1941 and pruned first in 1965 and more recently in 1984. The road divides at a curve; an extremely sharp curve is to the left. Here, you have an option for completing the loop. If continuing to the right, you will ascend through a loblolly pine plantation planted in 1950. At 1.15 miles on the right is a stand of pond pine (*Pinus serotina*), infrequent in this part of the state. You will pass a private house, to the left, and arrive at Hampton Road (SR-1603) at 1.6 miles. Turn left and follow Hampton Road 0.4 mile to a forest road on the left. You will enter a steel-blue gravel road at 2 miles, then pass a large, unique rock formation in the woods to the left. At 2.6 miles, you will reach a controlled forest burn, right and left; this is a bobwhite and quail management area. You will gradually descend; the Flat River is to the right. You will curve left, cross a tributary of the Flat River, and complete the loop at 3 miles. Turn right and return to the point of origin at State Forest Road at 3.8 miles.

The fourth walk is farther northeast. From the entrance of the third trail on State Forest Road, drive east 1 mile to Wilkins Road (SR-1613). Turn left and drive to the junction with Hampton Road. Follow Hampton Road to the left; after 0.2 mile, look for the forest road to the right. After entering the forest, you will notice open areas for the first 0.3 mile, then large hardwoods and pine. You will descend, cross a small stream, and ascend in a hardwood forest to a road fork at 0.4 mile. If continuing left, you will enter an area of natural forest reproduction, then a combination of oak species and Virginia yellow pine. Before reaching the gate and a dead end at 0.9 mile, you will pass through a rocky area and infrequently seen chestnut oak (*Quercus prinus*). Backtrack to the fork and turn left at 1.3 miles. You will descend to white pine planted in 1968. At 1.5 miles, you will pass an abandoned road (left) and ascend through mature loblolly pine. You will descend, then approach a timbered area at 2.1 miles. Turn right at a gravel forest road among saplings and wildflowers. You will arrive at a gate and Hampton Road at 2.3 miles. Turn right on Hampton Road and go 0.6 mile back to the trail's beginning, for a total hike of 2.9 miles. (USGS maps: Rougemont, Lake Michie)

Goodwin Forest, also part of the NCSU property, is in Moore County. Although it offers no developed trails, there are 4.1 miles of single-lane access roads open to hikers. If approaching from Carthage, go west on NC-22/24/27 for 1.3 miles to the junction with Bethlehem Church Road (SR-1261); turn left. After 1.5 miles, you will enter Goodwin Forest. Follow the first road to the left or go straight ahead. Permission for hiking is required from the College of Forest Resources, Department of Forestry, NCSU, Box 8002, Raleigh, NC 27695 (919-515-2891). (USGS map: Carthage)

# UNIVERSITY OF NORTH CAROLINA AT CHAPEL HILL
### Orange and Durham Counties

## North Carolina Botanical Garden

The 600-acre North Carolina Botanical Garden is a preserve of Southeastern trees, shrubs, plants, ferns, wildflowers, and herbs. Its nature trails are open daily; the administrative offices are open Monday through Friday. Guided tours of the garden are offered by prior arrangement to groups of 10 to 60 people.

The Totten Center is located across the street from the parking lot. Follow the signs on *North Carolina Botanical Garden Nature Trail*, a self-guided interpretive trail. You will cross a bridge at 0.2 mile and turn right. (Another trail ascends left to connect with other unnamed trails.) You will follow a combination of trails under a subcanopy of flowering trees such as dogwood and return to the parking lot after 1.5 miles.

*Address and Access:* North Carolina Botanical Garden, UNC-CH, CB# 3375 Totten Center, Chapel Hill, NC 27599 (919-962-0522). The garden is located in east Chapel Hill at Laurel Hill Road (SR-1901) 0.7 mile south of the junction of US-15/501 and NC-54.

## Penny's Bend Nature Preserve (Durham County)

This 84-acre nature preserve is upstream from Falls Lake on the north side of the Eno River. It is managed by the North Carolina Botanical Garden under a long-term lease from the Corps of Engineers. The preserve is unique because of its diabase geological structure and unusual vascular flora. The diabase is unerodable igneous rock that deflects the Eno River to form an oxbow shape. Within the bend's rocky river slope and soil ridge top are meadows with wildflowers more common to the prairies of the Midwest.

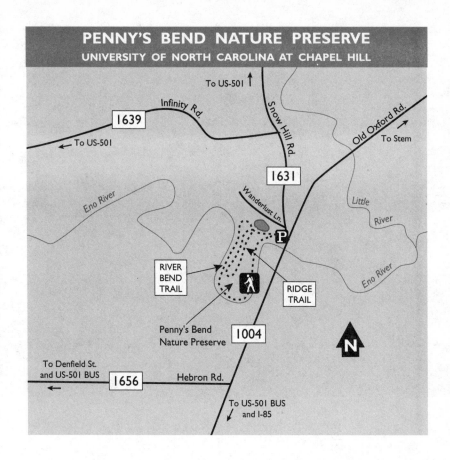

**PENNY'S BEND NATURE PRESERVE**
UNIVERSITY OF NORTH CAROLINA AT CHAPEL HILL

The preserve's history can be traced to the ancestral plantation of Duncan Cameron in the 1830s. Near the parking area of today's preserve is the site of Cameron's Mill, which served as a gristmill and sawmill. The rich grasslands within the river bend were excellent pasture for the Cameron family's livestock. The source of the bend's name is uncertain.

*Access:* From the junction of I-85 and US-15 Business (exit 177B if going west, exit 177C if going east), drive north on Roxboro Road for 1.3 miles and turn right on Old Oxford Road. After 3.3 miles, you will cross the Eno River bridge; turn immediately left to the parking lot on Snow Hill Road (SR-1631).

*University of North Carolina Botanical Gardens*

**River Bend Trail** *(1.8 miles, easy)*
**Ridge Trail** *(0.7 mile, easy)*

From the parking area, enter the preserve at the sign to enjoy the wildflower field stations. Some of the stations are for wild blue indigo (*Baptisia minor*), wild smooth coneflower (*Echinacea laevigata*), tall larkspur (*Delphinium exaltatum*), and hoary puccoon. Follow the trail into the woods and by the riverside to a fork at 0.1 mile. Stay left and follow the riverbank among dense oak, elm, walnut, and sycamore. At 1 mile is a huge grapevine. You will pass a rocky area on the right, then some river rapids. Turn right to ascend a rocky slope covered with wildflowers at 1.4 miles. You will then turn right at a woods road and enter a field; the caretaker's residence is to the left near a pond. At 1.6 miles, you will reach a junction with *Ridge Trail*, which forms a loop partly in the field to the right and along the ridge rim of the river. Continuing on *River Bend Trail*, you will pass under two large post oak trees, descend, and turn left at a fork at 1.7 miles. Return to the parking lot. (USGS map: Durham NE)

*Entrance to Falls Lake Trail, part of the Mountains-to-Sea Trail*

# Chapter 6

## MOUNTAINS-TO-SEA TRAIL

Mountains-to-Sea Trail (*MST*), a state trail, passes through the Triangle on its way from Clingmans Dome and the *Appalachian Trail* in Great Smoky Mountains National Park to the Nags Head area of the Atlantic coast. Of the proposed foot trail of more than 825 miles, segments totaling about 375 miles are finished. The major continuous segments are on federal property in the mountainous part of the state. The *MST* blaze is a white circle with a three-inch diameter.

On its passage through the Triangle, the *MST* follows *Falls Lake Trail* for 23.4 miles from NC-50 near the south side of the bridge over Falls Lake and ends at the Falls Lake dam (see the section on Falls Lake in chapter 1 for further information). Details of all the completed routes east and west of this point are included in *North Carolina Hiking Trails*, third edition, by Allen de Hart. Also, the North Carolina Division of Parks and Recreation has prepared a booklet, *An Introduction to North Carolina's* Mountains-to-Sea Trail, for distribution; call 919-846-9991. For the purposes of this guidebook, only an introduction to the history of the *MST* is included in this chapter.

After the North Carolina General Assembly passed the Trails System Act of 1973, the staff of the Department of Natural Resources and Community Development (DNRCD)—now the Department of Environment, Health, and Natural Resources (DEHNR)—began brainstorming about the future of trails. A catalyst was *Resources for Trails in North Carolina, 1972*, written by staff member Bob Buckner. With fresh ideas about trail purposes and usage, staff planners such as Alan Eaks and Jim Hallsey inspired others to move forward in implementing the Trails System Act. One of the act's statutes explains that "in order to provide for the ever-increasing outdoor recreation needs of an expanded population and in order to promote public access to, travel within, and enjoyment and appreciation of the outdoors, . . . trails should be established in natural scenic areas of the state, and in and near urban areas."

This was also a period when the trend for greenways was on the horizon. Regional councils and county governments were proposing canoe trails and trail connections, and Arch Nichols of the Carolina Mountain Club was proposing a 60-mile hiking trail from Mount Pisgah to Mount Mitchell. Discussing these and many other exciting ideas with the DNRCD staff was the North Carolina Trails Committee, a seven-member citizen advisory board.

The committee began functioning in January 1974 with Louise Chatfield of Greensboro as chair, followed by John Falter of Apex in 1976 and Dr. Doris B. Hammett of Waynesville in 1977. It was Dr. Hammett who led a planning committee for the Fourth National Trails Symposium, held at Lake Junaluska from September 7 to September 10, 1977. Among the distinguished speakers was Howard N. Lee, secretary of DNRCD and former mayor of Chapel Hill. Near the end of his speech, Lee said, "I think the time has come for us to consider the feasibility of establishing a state trail between the mountains and the seashore in North Carolina." He explained that he wanted the Trails Committee to plan a trail that would utilize the National Park Service, the United States Forest Service, state parks, city and county properties, and the property of private landowners "willing to give an easement over a small portion of their land on a legacy to future generations. I don't think we should be locked into the traditional concept of a trail with woods on both sides. . . . I think it would be a trail that would help— like the first primitive trails—bring us together. . . . It would depend on trail enthusiasts for maintenance. . . . Beyond that, how great it would be if other states would follow suit and that the state trails could be linked nationally." After the conference, Curtis Yates of the Department of Transportation (DOT) sent Lee a map of the *Mountains-to-Sea* bicycle trail, from Murphy to Manteo. Yates inquired if the bike trail could be part of the proposal.

Citizen task forces were established to design, negotiate easements for, construct, and maintain segments of the approximately 20-mile-wide corridor for the "dream trail," whose name became *Mountains-to-*

*Sea Trail*; the *to* was dropped for an easier abbreviation and to avoid the longer *MTST*. Its western trailhead would be at Clingmans Dome as a connector with the *Appalachian Trail* in Great Smoky Mountains National Park and its eastern trailhead at Nags Head on the Outer Banks. Between 1979 and 1981, the DNRCD signed cooperative planning agreements with the National Park Service, the United States Forest Service, and the United States Fish and Wildlife Service for the *MST* to pass through federal properties. Another agreement was signed in 1985 pledging a cooperative effort to share resources for the state's longest trail.

According to plans, the *MST* would use original trails in Great Smoky Mountains National Park to reach the Cherokee Indian reservation and the Blue Ridge Parkway. It would follow the Blue Ridge Parkway until reaching Nantahala National Forest, where it would alternate between the properties. It would also alternate between the Blue Ridge Parkway and Pisgah National Forest, with the exception of a long eastern curve into the Davidson River drainage of the Pisgah District and the Linville River and Wilson Creek drainages of the Grandfather District. On its return to the Blue Ridge Parkway at Mount Pisgah, it would follow the parkway's corridor to the Mount Mitchell entrance road before descending to Black Mountain Campground in the Toecane Ranger District of Pisgah National Forest. It would then return to the Blue Ridge Parkway for a short parallel before following Woods Mountain to US-221. From there, the *MST* would stay in the Grandfather District of Pisgah National Forest before returning to the Blue Ridge Parkway at Beacon Heights. It would then follow the parkway to its final eastern turn at the northern edge of Doughton Park.

From there, the *MST* would descend to Stone Mountain State Park, a section to be named in honor of Louise Chatfield (1920–86), a leader in the trails movement and founder of the North Carolina Trails Association in 1978. From Stone Mountain State Park, the *MST* route would enter private or public lands to Pilot Mountain State Park and Hanging Rock State Park. Continuing southeast to Lake Brandt, north of Greensboro, it would pass through Alamance and Durham Counties and approach Eno River State Park in Durham. From there, it would connect with the *Falls Lake Trail* system to Raleigh (see Chapter 1). From Raleigh, it would follow the floodplain corridor of the Neuse River through Johnston and Wayne Counties to Cliffs-of-the-Neuse State Park and through Lenoir County. It would leave the Neuse River to enter Croatan National Forest in Jones, Pamlico, and Carteret Counties. At Cedar Island, hikers would take a state ferry to Ocracoke, the beginning of the final 75 miles, and follow *Cape Hatteras Beach Trail* on the Outer Banks through Cape Hatteras National Seashore.

In addition to the main *MST* corridor across the state, regional connecting trails could be planned to major cities, Uwharrie National Forest, and other public areas such as state, city, and county parks. A specific route has not been defined. A footpath off the road would require the purchase or lease of nearly 400 miles of private property, the cost of which would make construction unlikely. A less visionary approach has been discussed among trail leaders since the beginning. This plan calls for a multiuse trail to include bike trails, horse trails, rail trails, and back-country roads. In metropolitan areas, sidewalks could be used.

Until a foot trail or a multiuse route is completed from the mountains to the sea, some hikers are choosing to see the state by biking the state's bike network. The longest route, the 700-mile *Mountains-to-Sea Bike Route #2*, is from Murphy to Manteo. It makes a junction with the *MST* foot trail at Balsam Gap at US-23/74 and the Blue Ridge Parkway. *Bike Route #2* follows the Blue Ridge Parkway to NC-181 east of Linville Falls and partway down the mountain, where the two mountains-to-sea trails cross for the last time in the mountains. For 129 miles along the Blue

*Falls Lake Trail, part of the*
*Mountains-to-Sea Trail*

Ridge Parkway, the *MST* plays tag with *Bike Route #2*, crisscrossing the parkway. Bikers are not allowed on the *MST* footpath if on Blue Ridge Parkway property, but hikers may walk the parkway between crossings. Another cross-state route is the 400-mile *North Line Trace* (*Highway Bike Route #4*), which runs close to Stone Mountain State Park, part of the proposed route of the *MST*. This route goes near at least three state parks and a number of county or town parks to Knotts Island. The 170-mile *Ocracoke Option* (Highway F) branches off the *Mountains-to-Sea* bike route west of Wilson at Christian Road (SR-1942) and goes to Cedar Island for the ferry trip to Ocracoke, the general route of the *MST* corridor.

The state's bicycle project began in the DOT in the early 1970s, the same decade that an enthusiastic awareness for statewide foot trails was promoted by the Division of Parks and Recreation. In 1974, Curtis Yates wrote a conceptual paper for a network of biking highways in the state, and Mary Meletiou assisted in the final draft to the state legislature. State Senator McNeill Smith of Greensboro introduced the bill, which easily passed as the North Carolina Bicycle and Bikeway Act of 1974. Both Yates and Meletiou have remained on the DOT staff for more than 20 years as leaders of the network project. Hikers who plan to supplement their passage across the state by biking may request information and maps from the Office of Bicycle and Pedestrian Transportation, DOT, Box 25201, Raleigh, NC 27611 (919-733-2804). There are 10 routes to choose from, for a total of 3,000 miles.

A few hikers have walked across the state on back roads near the *MST* corridor and short pieces of the state trail system. The first was Lee Price in 1982. Price's feat was sponsored by the North Carolina Trails Association. He began in Murphy and ended at Cape Hatteras National Seashore. Part of his trek was by bicycle. The most recent through-hike was made by Jeffrey Scott and Jarrett Franklin. They began October 18, 1994, at Nags Head and completed their journey on February 9, 1995, at Clingmans Dome. Of that time, 75 days were continuous backpacking. Graduates of Appalachian State University, they made their hike as part of a project to bring attention to preserving Howard's Knob at Boone.

In 1989, the Division of Parks and Recreation's trail staff produced "*Mountains-to-Sea Trail* Proposed Trail Routing and Plan of Action." Its purpose was to incorporate hiking, biking, horseback riding, and canoeing in the passage across the state. The proposal was never fully implemented because priority went to rail trails, greenways, and river trails; furthermore, the river trails cannot be contiguous. At the June 23 and September 15, 1995, meetings of the North Carolina Trails Committee, the subject was discussed again. The result was a motion by the committee to reaffirm the *MST* concept and encourage the state trails staff to open discussions with the DOT on working together in creating an arrangement of highway bike routes in sections where foot trails have not been completed.

# Appendix 1

## RESOURCE INFORMATION

The names and addresses listed below of national, state, and Triangle organizations associated with trails are intended to supplement those given in the text. For example, most greenway systems allow biking, and some streets and highways have bike routes. *Mountains-to-Sea Bike Route #2*, from Murphy to Manteo, passes northwest through Raleigh. Also, *Bike Route #1*, a north/south route from Virginia to South Carolina, contacts *Bike Route #2* in Raleigh. Because many hikers and walkers are bikers, information for bikers is included here. New residents of the Triangle may wish to know about trail clubs and special groups interested in outdoor activities.

### National Organizations

American Birding Association
Box 6599
Colorado Springs, CO 80934
719-634-7736

American Camping Association
5000 State Road, 67N
Martinsville, IN 46151
317-342-8456

American Hiking Society
Box 20160
Washington, DC 20041
703-385-3252

Appalachian Trail Conference
P.O. Box 807
Harpers Ferry, WV 25425
304-535-6331

Boy Scouts of America (national)
Box 152079
Irving, TX 75015
214-580-2000 (Call for information
   on state chapters.)

Friends of the Earth
218 D Street SE
Washington, DC 20003
202-544-2600

Girl Scouts of the USA
420 Fifth Avenue
New York, NY 10018
212-852-8000 (Call for information
on state chapters.)

National Wildlife Federation
1400 16th Street NW
Washington, DC 20036
202-797-6693

![marker]

## North Carolina Government Agencies

Department of Commerce, Travel,
and Tourism
430 North Salisbury Street
Raleigh, NC 27611
919-733-4171

Department of Environment,
Health, and Natural Resources
(DEHNR)
Box 27687
Archdale Building, 512 North
Salisbury Street
Raleigh, NC 27611
919-733-4984
*(Note that the state parks are in DEHNR but that the address and telephone number for the park superintendent, the trails director, and the regional trails specialist are as follows: Yorkshire Center, 12700 Bayleaf Church Road, Raleigh, NC 27614, 919-846-9991.)*

Department of Transportation
Bicycle Program
Box 25201
Raleigh, NC 27611
919-733-2804

Recreation Resources Service
Box 8004, NCSU
Raleigh, NC 27695
919-515-7118
*(For a fee, this office offers a detailed directory of municipal, county, college and university, military, national, and state parks, forests, and historic sites. Information on DEHNR offices and a number of professional organizations is included.)*

Wildlife Resources Commission
Archdale Building, 512 North
Salisbury Street
Raleigh, NC 27604
919-733-3391

![marker]

## North Carolina Citizens' Groups (chiefly in the Triangle area)

Appalachian Trail and Whitewater
Club
Box 3085
Louisburg, NC 27549
919-496-2521

Association for Preserving Eno
River Valley
4409 Guess Road
Durham, NC 27712

Carrboro Bicyclist Network
107 Mary Street
Carrboro, NC 27510
919-929-8671

Central Carolina Western Horse
  Association
10401 Lawrence Road
Wake Forest, NC 27587
919-520-2147

Duke Law School Hiking Club
5700 Barbee Chapel Road
Chapel Hill, NC 27514

Eno River Racers (cyclists)
900 West Main Street
Durham, NC 27701
919-544-3948

Friends of Mountains-to-Sea Trail
P.O. Box 3085
Louisburg, NC 27549
919-496-4771

Friends of State Parks
4202 Randleman Road
Greensboro, NC 27406

Governor's Council on Physical
  Fitness and Health
P.O. Box 267687
Raleigh, NC 27611
919-733-9615

NCSU Recreation Club
P.O. Box 8004, Biltmore Hall
Raleigh, NC 27695

Neuse Trails Association
170 Quail Drive
Dudley, NC 28333

North Carolina Bicycle Club
4908 Lily Atkins Road
Cary, NC 27611
919-851-9256

North Carolina Chapter of the
  Nature Conservancy
Suite 201, 4011 University Drive
Durham, NC 27707
919-403-8558

The North Carolina Fats Mountain
  Biking Club
P.O. Box 37725
Raleigh, NC 27627
919-876-3599

North Carolina Horse Council
P.O. Box 12999
Raleigh, NC 27605
919-821-1030

North Carolina Rail Trails
703 Ninth Street, Suite 124
Durham, NC 27705
919-493-6394

North Carolina Wesleyan College
  Bicycle Club
Wesleyan College Station
Rocky Mount, NC 27801
919-977-7171

North Carolina Wildflower Preservation Society
708 Brent Road

Raleigh, NC 27606
919-859-1187

North Raleigh Mountain Biking
  Association
520 Brittany Bay West
Raleigh, NC 27614
919-846-8198

Outing Club of Duke University
Office of Student Affairs
101-3 Bryan Center
Duke University
Durham, NC 27706

Raleigh All-Star Cycling Club
4108 Darlington Road
Raleigh, NC 27612
919-783-6653

Sierra Club (Capital Group)
Box 4845, 230 Hillsboro Road
Cary, NC 27519
919-481-1707

Sierra Club (Headwaters Group)
58 Newton Drive
Durham, NC 27707
919-490-1566

Sierra Club (Medoc Group)
318 Breedlove Road
Nashville, NC 27856
919-459-4502

Sierra Club (Orange-Chatham
  Group)
407 Sharon Road
Chapel Hill, NC 27514
919-942-2273

Triangle Greenways Council
Triangle J Council of Governments
P.O. Box 12276
Research Triangle Park, NC 27709

Triangle Land Conservancy
1100A Wake Forest Road
Raleigh, NC 27604
919-833-3662
  *(An alternate address and phone
  number are Triangle Land Conservancy, P.O. Box 13031, Research Triangle Park, NC 27709, 919-833-3662.)*

Triangle Rails-to-Trails Conservancy
P.O. Box 13000
Research Triangle Park, NC 27709
919-461-1205

Triangle Trailblazers (Volkswalkers)
4804 East Tapers Drive
Raleigh, NC 27694
919-873-9950

UNC-Chapel Hill Outing Club
Box 16, Carolina Union, 065-A
Chapel Hill, NC 27514

Wake County Audubon Society
111 Winding Ridge Drive
Cary, NC 27511

*For additional and updated informa-
tion, request the Directory of Trail
Associations and Trail Managing
Agencies in North Carolina from
Trails Directory, 12700 Bay Leaf
Church Road, Raleigh, NC 27614-
9633 (919-846-9991).*

# Appendix 2

## SPECIAL TRAILS

A few trails in the Triangle area have been specially constructed for use by the physically disabled. Additionally, some greenways, by the nature of their smooth asphalt paving, are adaptable for wheelchair usage. Examples of these special trails are *Big Lake Handicapped Trail* in William B. Umstead State Park; *Black Creek Trail* and *Swift Creek Trail* in Cary; *Ironwood Trail, Walnut Creek Trail, Buckeye Trail,* and the trail for the handicapped in Blue Jay Point County Park in Raleigh; the south section of *North/South Trail* and the north section of *Rock Quarry Trail* by the Vietnam War memorial in Durham; and *Trail for the Handicapped* in Greencroft Gardens near Louisburg.

Hikers who wish a special place for primitive or full-service camping will find primitive walk-in campsites or water, electricity, and asphalt parking pads for RVs at the following: Jordan Lake, Falls Lake, John H. Kerr Dam and Reservoir, Cedarock Park, Clemmons Educational State Forest, Eno River State Park, Medoc Mountain State Park, Raven Rock State Park, San-Lee Park, and William B. Umstead State Park.

Interpretive trails are a favorite for families with children. Usually, these special trails have brochures and/or signs for plants and wildlife. Examples are as follows:

American Beech Nature Trail
Bentonville Battleground History Trail
Bond Nature Trail
Clemmons Talking Tree Trail
East Bluff Trail
Eno Nature Trail
Fallon Creek Trail

Fox Creek Nature Trail
Frances Liles Interpretive Trail
Greencroft Lake Trail
Henderson Nature Trail
North Carolina Botanical Garden Nature Trail
Old Beech Nature Trail
Shepherd Nature Trail
West Bluff Trail
White Oak Nature Trail
Wildlife Observation Trail
Woodland Nature Trail

# TRAIL INDEX